NIGO®

From Japan with Love

the DESIGN MUSEUM

From Japan with Love

Edited by Rachel Hajek and Esme Hawes

Contents

Foreword

NIGO is a cultural phenomenon – a world-class fashion designer and a creative director, a trendsetter from street to runway, a DJ and record producer, an entrepreneur and collector. His roots are in Japan but his frames of reference are global, as is his reputation. His creative journey began as a teenager in the 1980s when he began to amass a collection of objects, particularly childhood ephemera and clothes from post-war America, which now numbers in excess of 10,000 items. Collecting fuelled his creative vision, and in turn he has become one of the most collected of fashion designers; collaborations have ranged across the cultural spectrum with companies from Nike to Nintendo, and with individual designers and artists from KAWS to Virgil Abloh and Pharell Williams.

This publication accompanies the first museum exhibition exploring NIGO's work, his inspirations and his ongoing impact. Radical and impactful design underpins everything NIGO does, from NOWHERE and A Bathing Ape, to his output as KENZO's first ever Japanese creative director since its founder Kenzō Takada. From the outset, as he observed recently, 'I wanted to do it properly'. He was driven by an energy Pharrell Williams describes as one of 'restless metamorphosis … and constant evolution'.

The Design Museum exhibition and this book survey this constantly evolving career over four sections, starting with NIGO's teenage bedroom and culminating with his current engagement with Japanese craft and rituals.

As befits one of the most inventive of design collaborators, the project is a collaboration between the curatorial team, led by Rachel Hajek and Esme Hawes, and NIGO and his studio. We also thank NOT A HOTEL as the headline sponsor of the exhibition, for helping to bring a much-anticipated show to the UK and for the beautifully crafted tearoom in the exhibition's last section. Above all, though, we thank and pay tribute to NIGO. He has been a generous lender and collaborator, whose creative energy and vision we are proud to be exploring and celebrating at the Design Museum in London and beyond.

NIGO outside the Design Museum, London, with a model of the museum on his head, 2026.

A Conversation: NIGO with Johanna Agerman Ross

After a tour of NIGO's collection of clothing, magazines, furniture and film posters, we end up in a room in the back of his Tokyo studio. Here stands a small tearoom, only two *tatami* mats in size. Outside the tearoom entrance, in the place where you would normally find a stone, is a manhole cover from Chandigarh, designed by the Swiss architect Le Corbusier. Perched on its roof is a wooden bird, the same that American designers Ray and Charles Eames used to have in their LA living room. NIGO slides open a door and hops in to demonstrate its function, swiftly moving, in a kneeling position, across the mats. He shows how an adjacent galley kitchen is used for preparation ahead of the tea ceremony. A custom hatch has been added to facilitate passing utensils from the kitchen. It's a NIGO original. Just like so many of the other things he surrounds himself with, it's witty and a little quirky, well-loved and deeply personal. It's clear this is a place of refuge as well as inspiration – a place to be uniquely NIGO.

JAR
When did you start collecting?

NIGO
My collection of 1950s fashion started in my teens in the 1980s. I got into 1950s fashion through a Japanese band called The Checkers. I was a big fan of theirs, and they wore vintage Americana. For me, there's always a key element of fashion that comes from music. I remember getting this pair of Levi's jeans and a white T-shirt and that's where it all started from – but even before then, I was fascinated with objects. The very first thing I remember collecting was a small Donald Duck figurine that I got in a *fukubukuro* bag, like a lucky-dip shopping bag full of things, that my parents bought me for New Year's. I still have the figurine.

JAR
And where did you find the fashion pieces at a young age?

NIGO
First, I bought things new but then this vintage clothes trend started in Japan with a lot of Americana coming into the market and vintage stores opening and selling 1950s stuff. The funny thing is, young people today are doing the same thing – looking back thirty years in time, as they're buying stuff from the 1990s.

JAR
Have you kept everything that you have bought over the years?

NIGO
Yeah, pretty much everything. I have actually worn most of the clothes myself, so they're all my size.

JAR
And your collection is still growing. Where do you source things nowadays?

NIGO
I usually purchase from a dealer in America. But I don't do trades directly with a dealer, because once they find out it's me, they'll try to raise the price. When I have the time, I also enjoy going to vintage stores myself in Koenji.

JAR
How come collecting is such an important creative process for you?

NIGO
There's a famous Japanese pottery master named Rosanjin, and he used to collect a lot of things. He used to say that the things he collected were his teachers. And I feel the same way. I collect all these things, and looking at the objects there are details that I notice and new ideas that come from that. So I feel I learn a lot from just looking at objects, and in that sense I feel kindred with Rosanjin.

JAR
Looking at your archive and your studio, there seems to have been a shift in your collecting interests in recent years. You started with Americana and popular culture, as well as design pieces by Jean Prouvé and Ray and Charles Eames, but now it seems that you are looking more towards Japanese traditional crafts. Would that be a correct reading?

NIGO
Yes, you're correct. I have already learned a lot from my collection of vintage American and

European pieces, and at one point I was starting to feel like I hadn't seen anything new when collecting and looking at things from overseas. So, one day around fifteen years ago, my wife suggested that I come and see *kabuki* theatre with her. I had no interest at that time, but I went with her and I was shocked because everything from the costumes to the backdrops had colour combinations I had never seen before; I realised that maybe there's a lot to learn from Japanese traditional culture. I have always been into analogue things, and I realised that *kabuki* is very analogue – it's purely people performing, it's not about flashy lights and stage constructions, so it really resonated with me.

JAR
You studied media rather than fashion at Bunka Fashion College, what did you take away from that?

NIGO
NIGO never smiles.

JAR
A lesson you have taken seriously, but what about the creative process?

NIGO
I learned about editing, and that's something that I have put to use in all of my work with clothes. But I never had proper teaching in either music or fashion, the fields I have focused my work on. Instead, I developed my knowledge and interest out of my love for these disciplines. Street culture is now mainstream, but when I started, no one cared and no one knew about it. People were asking 'What are you doing?'. That was the reaction I was getting.

JAR
Do you remember the moment of change in people's attitudes?

NIGO
I opened a store in the back streets of Harajuku in 1993 with Jun Takahashi, who I met at Bunka. It was because we didn't have any money that we picked the back streets, as we couldn't afford a store on the main streets of Harajuku. But then, soon after, other stores started to open and then by 1997 and 1998 the place became known as Ura-Harajuku – the hidden Harajuku – and what we had created became Ura-Hara culture. We had a lot of international customers visiting us back then; people like Virgil Abloh came. But in doing this it wasn't like I set a goal or that I had the intention to do something like that. I was just doing something I loved.

JAR
How does the process of creation work for you?

NIGO
It's kind of like catching air, I guess. Not an easy thing to define!

JAR
But is it about conversation, drawing, sampling?

NIGO
Until recently, such as when I created collections for HUMAN MADE, I would take vintage pieces from my archive and get inspiration from them, so I would work from what's already there. But since I've been working with the KENZO team in Paris, there's been a lot about communicating ideas verbally and giving them visual references

that the team can create samples from. So recently my creative process has evolved, but it's also kind of two separate processes, two different ways of doing things.

JAR
Would you say that the creative process is teamwork?

NIGO
At KENZO I feel like a team leader, guiding the team members. For HUMAN MADE I have done a lot of the work myself, but recently, since working with the KENZO team in Paris, I have started thinking that working with a team is a good way to nurture the next generation of artists.

JAR
Without formal training in fashion or pattern-cutting, you have managed to create some groundbreaking forms within clothing and retail. It's an amazing feat, but how have you approached it?

NIGO
I like the Japanese term *katayaburi*, which means to break out of the box. But, in order to break out of that box, you need to know the box. So I always learn the basics for anything I do, and then I move away from it or change the details of something. People might think it's weird or strange, but I can handle that because I feel I know what I'm doing by knowing the box. If I was approaching these things and making these changes without having that knowledge, just changing things for the sake of it or because I was trying to create something trendy that changes things, that would be embarrassing.

The creative journey is in the process, and I always think that things can't be too simple or too easy. There's another Japanese word, from Japanese martial arts philosophy, *shuhari*, which speaks of the process of learning and how you fully master something. You start with *Shu*, to learn to follow or obey the rules, then you have to break them, *Ha*, and finally you have to make it into your own, *Ri*. This is something that I apply in many of the things I do, from fashion to music and now to the tea ceremony.

JAR
In being so closely involved with creating a retrospective exhibition about your work, what do you think is important to communicate to people who will come and see it?

NIGO
That what I started was very small, but it turned into something mainstream, even major. But it hasn't been easy, to make something from nothing really, so I like to show people how deep it is, how much history there is to what I've done and how important the references of my archive are to me and my practice. Because people think it's easy to create some of this stuff, that it's superficial, but for me it's really deep, a deep engagement with objects of the past to create something new. It also seems like a good thing to do at this point in time when people are getting less interested in actual objects and live more and more through the virtual. The physical object is key for me. Even with music, it's a different experience if you listen to a digital file compared to on a CD or a vinyl. You listen to the album from start to finish – you don't skip the songs or listen to an AI-generated playlist. It's a different experience, and there's an importance in that tactile experience.

NIGO at the Design Museum, 2026.

Introduction

In recent decades, the role of the creative director has increasingly grown in importance within the creative industries. Looking at the major trends and shifts within retailing, marketing, luxury and popular culture at large, behind much of today's standard practice are just a select few powerful individuals. Known to the world as NIGO, he is one of these remarkable figures. He has been shaping youth and contemporary culture for over thirty years, with a multifaceted practice that covers fashion, design, music production, interior design, brand building, and – underpinning everything – creative direction. His is a craft honed through an obsession with, and collecting of, all manner of design.

From founding his first fashion brand, A Bathing Ape, to currently leading KENZO as the fashion house's artistic director, the impact of NIGO's career is significant. A master of sampling and collaboration, he has produced some of the most influential ideas, designs and trends in recent style and fashion history, inspiring a devoted worldwide following. Referred to by his peers as 'the general', he always has his finger on the pulse of youth culture. In the 1990s he began 'quoting' key cultural references from hip-hop, skate, sci-fi and beyond, connecting to like-minded audiences who have remained loyal fans ever since. Beyond the design of individual garments, NIGO builds entire brand universes. Extending from stores are eateries, music, events – even hair salons. He doesn't just

The fashion-conscious teenager. NIGO in his bedroom.

offer the T-shirt, but a whole lifestyle. Every detail contributes to a total vision, from concept to consumer. His approach to design has become a business model that many strive to replicate.

This publication is the first to trace NIGO's creative progression, from Americana-besotted teenager to training to become a master of the Japanese tea ceremony. Continually evolving, he has turned his hand to an eclectic portfolio of projects. With each venture he studies deeply, absorbs, refines and innovates, always building upon what he has previously created. Throughout his rise from humble beginnings in the city of Maebashi in the Kantō region to internationally renowned creative director, one constant that has underpinned NIGO's journey is his passion for collecting. He has kept and meticulously archived possessions from his childhood and formative teenage years, as well as throughout his adult career. NIGO's astonishing 10,000-plus piece collection spreads across multiple floors of his Tokyo studio, and forms the basis of everything he does. Vintage denim sits beside *Star Wars* figurines, while his first business cards remain just as precious as his Jean Prouvé furniture. This treasured archive is a constant source of inspiration and mentorship for his craft – a live toolbox from which he continually draws.

NIGO at the opening of the Billionaire Boys Club flagship store, 28 November 2007, New York.

Published to coincide with the first ever retrospective of NIGO's work, at London's Design Museum, this book celebrates his vision and legacy. For both exhibition and book, NIGO granted special access to his archive, offering a unique visual window into his enticing universe. Whatever you discover in NIGO's world, it is always from Japan, and with love.

NIGO's record collection at his house in Shibuya, Tokyo.

DES
MU

NIGO at the Design Museum, 2026.

The Future is in the Past

W. David Marx

The surrealist filmmaker Luis Buñuel liked to quote an artistic maxim from the Catalonian philosopher Eugenio d'Ors: 'What doesn't grow out of tradition is plagiarism.' This statement can seem paradoxical at first, but Buñuel and the other avant-garde artists understood that significant acts of creative invention are not pulled from a pure imagination but can be seen as 'answers' to previous work. Expertise in the existing canon always offers hints about *what* to create as well as *what not* to create in order to avoid banal repetition.

NIGO in his bedroom, 1980s. The wardrobe is now part of his collection (see page 38).

Born Tomoaki Nagao, in 1970, the Japanese designer and creative director NIGO is one of the strongest practitioners to anchor their creative acts in deep historical knowledge. 'The Future is in the Past' has become an unofficial motto for NIGO's clothing brand HUMAN MADE – and, based on the company's recent successes, this creative strategy seems to meet the demands of twenty-first-century global consumers. NIGO's two-decade creative partnership with music producer/creative director Pharrell Williams culminated in a joint collection for Louis Vuitton Men's line in January 2025. Later that year, HUMAN MADE made an initial public offering on the Tokyo Stock Exchange at a $460 million market capitalisation.

A teenage NIGO, wearing an International Stüssy Tribe stadium jacket.

But NIGO's influence goes beyond his own projects. The most dynamic brands in global consumer culture – ranging from athletic gear manufacturers to storied European luxury houses – have adopted the specific merchandising techniques that NIGO pioneered during the 1990s. It is no hyperbole to say that NIGO ended up inventing the 'future' of fashion for the twenty-first century. He could only do this through a deep understanding of, and respect for, the past.

As much as NIGO is an important source of global creativity, he is also a world-class collector.

HUMAN MADE T-shirt with 'the Future is in the Past' graphic (white colourway).

HUMAN MADE T-shirt with 'the Future is in the Past' graphic (black colourway).

His archive exists across multiple apartments and warehouses. There are elements of Japanese culture that seem to have influenced his desire to accumulate so much. Beginning in the late 1970s, the Japanese *otaku* subculture bubbled up into mainstream culture from manga and anime fans who proved their love of a certain series through the obsessive hoarding of related products. As the Japanese economy exploded in the 1980s, this monomaniacal consumer behaviour extended to nearly every product category, from fashion to music to cars. In particular, young men interested in American vintage clothing used a strengthening yen to visit the US and buy up rare deadstock and second-hand garments.

NIGO spent his early teenage years right in the midst of this Americana craze. Japan was also undergoing a 1950s rock revival, which gave NIGO a life-long love for Buddy Holly and post-war toys. He began to collect vintage Levi's jackets and jeans during his weekend pilgrimages to Tokyo's Harajuku shopping district. In the late 1980s, he looked up to DJ/tastemaker Hiroshi Fujiwara, whose personal connections to London's iconic Malcolm McLaren and Vivienne Westwood made him a pioneering evangelist of punk and American hip-hop in Japan. Once NIGO moved to Tokyo to attend Bunka Fashion College, he joined Fujiwara's clique and was soon styling celebrities, writing columns for fashion magazines, and DJing at clubs. In 1993 he started his own clothing store, NOWHERE, in Harajuku, in collaboration with his friend Jun Takahashi of the brand UnderCover.

When NIGO decided to create an original clothing line for NOWHERE, he tapped into aesthetics straight from his personal archive. The clothes' graphics played with the iconography from American sci-fi: films such as *Planet of the*

Apes, *2001: A Space Odyssey* and *Star Wars* (all of which dabbled in 'future past' aesthetics). Early garments replicated his favourite vintage and American outdoor gear. These influences all came together in a moment of era-defining inspiration during a buying trip to Maine in 1993. NIGO had woken up with jetlag in the very early morning and decided to visit the 24-hour L.L.Bean. Sitting down in a chair, he looked up and saw a stylish camouflage hanging on the wall. This design later became the starting point for his Ape Head camo – arguably one of the most iconic design motifs of the late 1990s and early 2000s.

The front façade of the original NOWHERE store, Harajuku shopping district, Tokyo. Inside, wire netting split the shop in two to showcase the very different styles of NIGO and Jun Takahashi.

Interior of the 1998 NOWHERE (BUSY WORK SHOP) store, Harajuku, Tokyo. Designed by Wonderwall.

As NIGO's brand grew, he bought up a host of rarer vintage items, while also forging significant innovations in how to merchandise his new products. He turned the Andy Warhol concept on its head – rather than displaying consumer products as art pieces in a gallery, he presented consumable commercial products as if they were artworks in ultra-clean retail spaces. Designed by Wonderwall's Masamichi Katayama, the stores set a new template for global high-end consumption over the next few decades. The notoriously long lines outside NIGO's shops motivated Nike and other global brands to hire veterans of the Japanese and British streetwear scenes to bring the same magic into the mass market.

With his second major company, HUMAN MADE, in the 2010s, NIGO moved even deeper into the exploration of archival designs. Alongside items such as rare Levi's and Lee jeans, NIGO's personal archive also contains entire categories of goods wholly unknown today, such as candy-bar salesmen jackets and collegiate blank-canvas 'beer jackets' on which the wearer would ask friends to scribble their names in marker. HUMAN MADE has created new versions of both styles, which arguably have set fashion trends for our current era.

In this way, NIGO's attitude towards his archive is not pure Confucianism – namely, the belief that greatness *only* exists in the past and requires returning to the rituals of an earlier age. As much as NIGO respects past manufacturing, his designs are rarely pure reproductions of previous forms; they twist the best of the past to find something that meets our present moment. But no amateur could do such work. This entire creative process requires an intense depth of knowledge. In being one of the few people alive who knows almost every casual garment that has ever existed, NIGO can pull things from the archive that contemporary consumers will not recognise, and will therefore treat as novel.

At the same time, NIGO's knowledge is never superficial. He is not an *otaku*, mindlessly buying up things because he is a hoarder or completist. He is an expert curator, and his knowledge includes the contextual information for each garment. This provides him with a clear model for how to make new goods that *mean something*. In the age before our sprawling post-modern global consumer economy, each piece of clothing took its import from its particular position within a social milieu. NIGO has learned this from his archive, and it is no coincidence that he has been able to tap familiarity with the past to make new garments that mean so much to people today – and will surely do so in the future, as well.

The following pages explore highlights from NIGO's extensive collection – ranging from items in his teenage bedroom to vintage clothing and accessories – and show how his archival eye has inspired his work over the decades.

LEVI'S 507XX – the first Levi's item that NIGO ever bought. This is Levi's second model, from 1986. 'It cost 38,000 Japanese yen at the time. I told my mother I bought it for 3,800 yen, but she was still very upset (probably the most upset I have ever seen her).'

Donald Duck push puppet. NIGO was bought this in a New Year's Happy Bag when he was five years old. 'This is my first collection item.'

Felix the Cat moneybank, 1983. 'I really wanted to purchase a vintage coin bank, but I could only find brand new ones. But it's funny how this has now turned into vintage.'

NIGO also collected vintage AV equipment. This Philco vacuum tube TV is from 1959, and still functions.

Sugar RT-SW7 red radio cassette player

SG-100 graphic equalizer, Aurex stereo amplifier model and Aurex AT-1000MK II audio digital timer. This stereo system belonged to NIGO's brother.

Aurex SR-P5F direct-drive turntable. Owned by NIGO's brother, this sat on top of the Aurex sound system on the previous page.

Technics Quartz SL-1200 MK2 direct-drive turntable. The Technics SL-1200 was a favourite of hip-hop DJs, allowing for new techniques like scratching. As NIGO could only afford to own one turntable, he would borrow his brother's turntable (the one in the above photo), without his permission for early mixing experiments.

This Bombeat RT-S71D radio cassette player belonged to NIGO's brother

Beat Master CMX-5500 DJ mixer

'Cassette tapes that I listened to at the time. I dubbed them from rental records, and typed the labels myself.'

‘At home there were old drum sets that my father used. I wanted new ones, but I couldn’t afford it, so I gathered catalogues from every drum maker I could find and stared at them.’

White varsity jacket, Troop, 1980s. Cult hip-hop clothing label Troop emerged in the late 1980s in New York, and became known for their distinctive leather and varsity-style jackets.

Pile bucket hat, Kangol, 1980s

Clock pendant, Dalico, 1980s. 'This is actually a shower clock, but I wore it as fashion.'

'Orb & Polka Dot' jeans, Vivienne Westwood, Spring/Summer 1986. These jeans are from Vivienne Westwood's 1986 Mini-Crini collection, known for its playful prints and reinterpretation of Victoriana.

'John Bull' hat, Vivienne Westwood, Autumn/Winter 1987. This black felt hat is from Vivienne Westwood's 1987 Harris Tweed collection for which she 'utilised convention to make things unorthodox'.

At the 2014 Grammys, Pharrell Williams famously wore a version of Westwood's 'Mountain Hat', designed for the 1982 Nostalgia of Mud collection

'Deep Sky' blazer, Vivienne Westwood, Autumn/Winter 1987. This blazer is from Westwood's 1987 Harris Tweed collection.

In the photo of NIGO in his bedroom as a teenager (see page 18), this horse and gumby doll can be seen on the shelf

Ceramic salt and pepper shakers

NIGO first saw these Beatles figurines in *Olive* magazine. 'When I moved to Tokyo, I found them at the Bunkaya Zakkaten store and bought them.'

Framed poster: artwork by Japanese illustrator Eizin Suzuki, titled *American Portrait*, 1982

This was the first non-Japanese record that NIGO bought, when he was in 7th grade. 'I didn't know who Buddy Holly was at the time – I bought it just from looking at the album cover, because it was cool.'

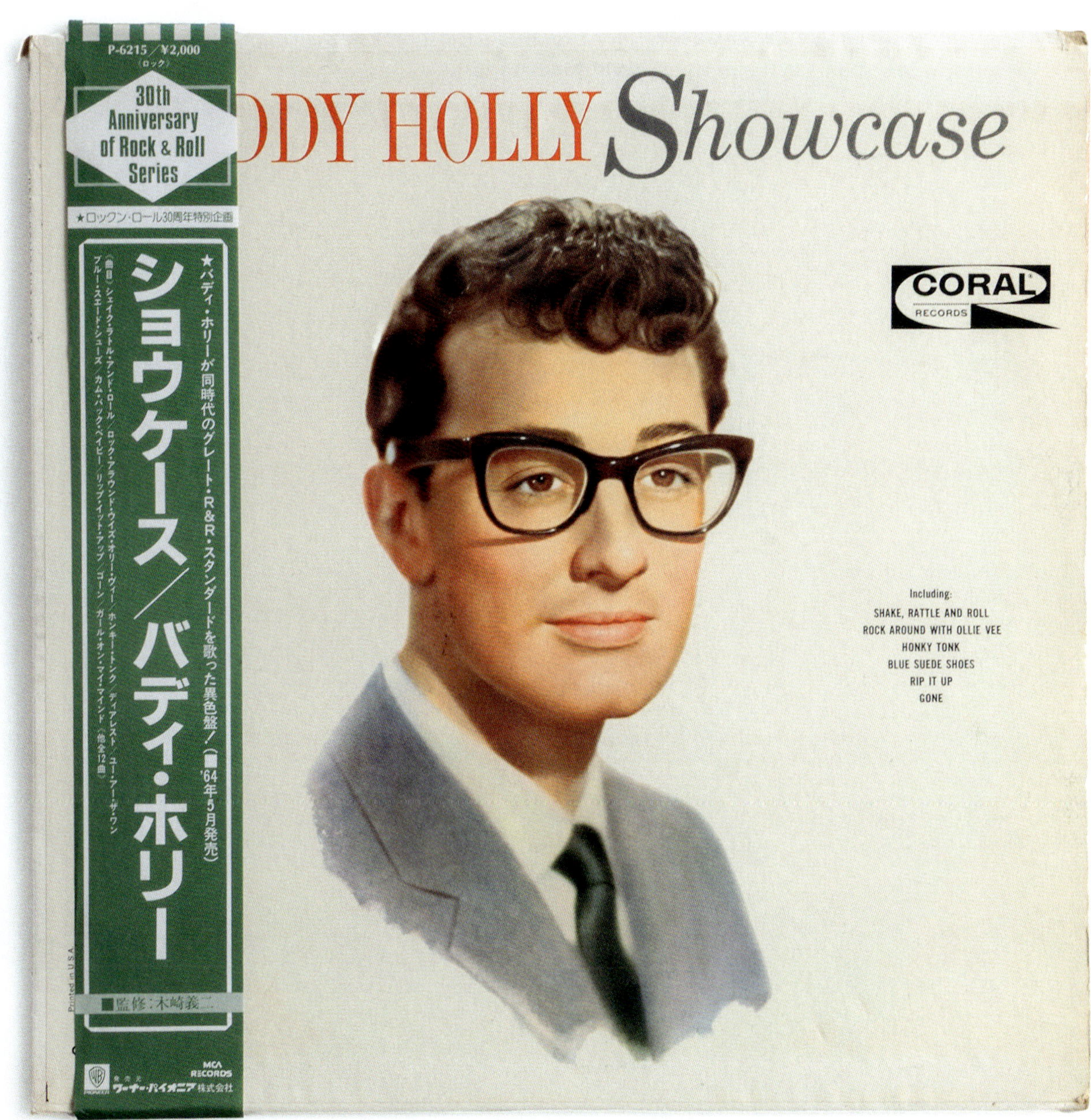

In his first year at junior high school, NIGO became obsessed with the Japanese pop-rock band The Checkers after his girlfriend introduced him to their music. He was drawn to their 1950s American rockabilly look.

Long sleeve T-shirt, Boys' Life, 1980s. 'This is a brand 45RPM, which Checkers members used to wear all the time.'

NIGO's home-recorded video tapes of The Checkers

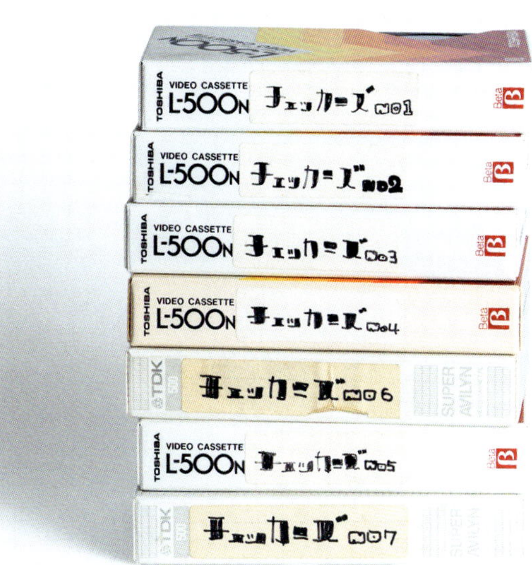

Merchandise for The Checkers: T-shirt and rosette

High school notebook. The drawing on the right shows NIGO's dream bedroom layout. On the cover of the notebook, he drew a mirror he wanted that he had seen in a magazine.

NIGO bought this mirror when he came to live in Tokyo. It was the exact mirror he had drawn on the cover of his school notebook.

When considering his options after high school, NIGO first looked at the London-based Saint Martin's School of Art. But his parents were worried about NIGO living alone overseas, and instead encouraged him to think about options closer to home. With this in mind, NIGO turned to the prestigious Bunka Fashion College in Tokyo.

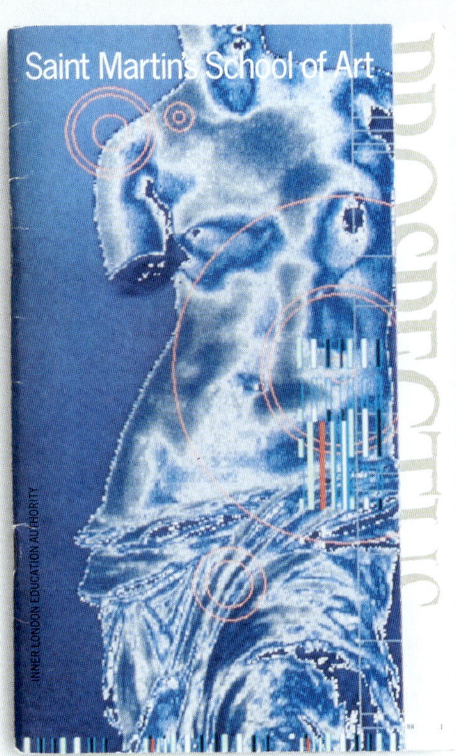

NIGO's skateboard. Steve Caballero Cab Chinese Dragon skateboard deck from around 1986; artwork by Vernon Courtlandt Johnson (VCJ)

Olive magazines. NIGO describes this magazine as his early fashion bible.

Clothing tags, collected by NIGO from clothes that he bought in the 1980s

Kung fu shoes. 'There was a Kung fu boom in Japan. But as a fashion item, I bought these for about 500 Japanese yen.'

Martial arts magazines. The front cover seen here features the film *Kids From Shaolin*, from 1984.

Master Cloth chore jacket with heart-shaped buttons, Carhartt, 1930s. Carhartt jackets were designed to be extremely robust, with big pockets, reinforced stitching and removable buttons.

Whizit dungarees, Lee, 1927. One of NIGO's favourite and rarest pieces in his collection, these popular workwear overalls were the first to use a zipper rather than hook fasteners. Lee held a contest to name the dungarees. The winning name was 'Whizit' – a reference to the sound of their new zipper.

Bing Crosby's denim jacket, Levi's, 1950s. After a long day hunting, American singer and actor Bing Crosby was denied entry to the Vancouver Hotel due to his double denim outfit. Levi's grasped the PR opportunity and made Crosby this tuxedo jacket. The incident propelled denim into the spotlight, coining the term 'Canadian Tuxedo' to refer to double denim.

Sukajan (souvenir jacket), 1950s. American GIs stationed at the Yokosuka Naval Base near Tokyo commissioned jackets from local craftspeople to commemorate their tours of duty – *sukajan* is a contraction of 'Yokosuka jumper'. Early *sukajan* were often made with repurposed kimono fabric or parachute silk. Following a varsity jacket style, and often reversible, they usually combined Japanese-inspired embroidery of cherry blossoms, tigers or dragons with maps and military motifs. By the 1960s, Japanese youth adopted the *sukajan* as a symbol of rebellion, with popular movies associating the style with gangsters.

Floral print souvenir jacket, 1950s. This jacket uses *nishijin-ori*, an artisanal woven silk used for traditional kimono. Its use for a souvenir jacket is exceptionally rare.

Memorial jacket, Workman's Manufacturing Co, 1930s

hlorophyll

These work caps were made from around the 1930s to the 1960s, and are recognisable as part of NIGO's everyday personal style

Buddy Lee dolls were made by the workwear brand Lee between 1920 and 1962. Initially a promotional tool, they quickly became a best-selling toy. Originally they were made from composition (sawdust, glue and other materials). NIGO has a collection of over 100 of these earlier examples. Production in plastic began in the 1940s.

'Whizits' advertising sign, Lee, 1920s. NIGO's HUMAN MADE label pays homage to the 'Union Made' motif, which was introduced in the early 20th century to signal products made by unionised workers.

Lamb Knit Sweaters papier-mâché mascot, 1930s–40s

Levis wooden advertising, 1940–50s

Railroad books and matchstick boxes: W.M. Finck & Co., Carhartt and Sweet-Orr, 1920s–40s

Shirt, BIGMAC, 1980s

T-shirts in packaging, Hanes, 1980s

501 jeans. 'This is the first pair of jeans I bought, when I was in 9th grade (fifteen years old). I remember trying on 27 32 (1 inch smaller than the one I actually bought), because they shrink to fit.'

'Clothing and accessories from Hollywood Ranch Market – still one of my favorite stores to this day.'

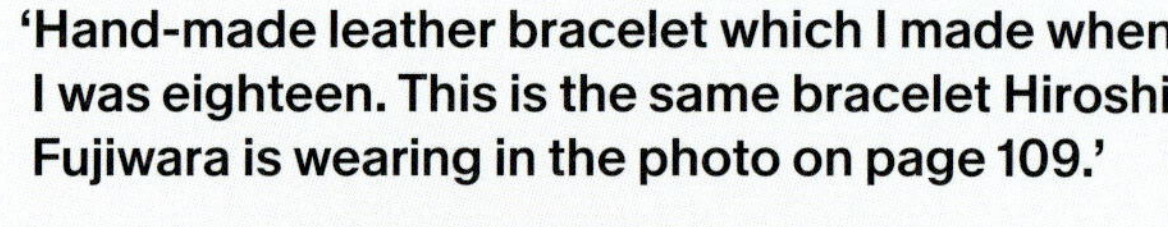
'Hand-made leather bracelet which I made when I was eighteen. This is the same bracelet Hiroshi Fujiwara is wearing in the photo on page 109.'

Cap for Kintetsu Buffaloes, a baseball team from Osaka, Japan, 1970s

‘Wearing denim and a white T-shirt, plus these glasses, was my usual style as a teenager.’

Black framed glasses, Shady Character, 1980s. ‘This was the Audrey Hepburn model from *Breakfast at Tiffany’s*.’

‘I wanted Converse when I was in 5th or 6th grade, but my mother said they were too expensive and instead bought me these American Wolf Sneakers. My older brother was wearing real Converse, however.’

‘When I was in 7th grade, I bought myself a real pair of Converse. (I saved up my New Year’s money and my allowance.)’

Nike backpack. 'My brother's hand-me-down that I used. All my friends used ASICS but I believed NIKE was cooler.'

NIGO's skiing jacket. 'Skiing was the only sport I ever did, and I reached a high skill level. I wore this killy jacket not just for skiing, but as fashion as well.'

Mr. Peanut sweatshirt, Planters, 1980s.
NIGO wore this sweatshirt as a teenager.

Mr. Peanut toy trucks, Planters, 1980s

NIGO bought British footwear from brands including Dr. Martens and the boutique Robot, located on King's Road, Chelsea, in the 1980s. This style of shoe, known as 'beetle crushers' or 'creepers', is associated with various subcultures including Teddy Boys and punks.

At the age of seventeen, NIGO had a part-time job in a factory that made headphones for Sony. Using his young person's train pass, he would travel into Tokyo to attend shifts. He spent his pay cheques on vintage clothes, records and magazines.

Superhero Go-ranger poster and figures. 'My favourite was Blue Ranger. There was a live action show being performed at the top of a department store. I went and got their autograph.'

Honda Roller Through GoGo scooter, 1970s

'My favorite Denjin Zaborger toy. I played with it so much, and that's how it got broken.'

Cash register toy, Aster, 1960s

Small World block toys, Lorenz Holz Spiel, 1970s

Superhero figures, based on Japanese TV superheroes from the 1970s and 1980s

Tin toys, 1970s

Aesop's Fables Picture Cubes, 1970s

Microman robot toys in boxes, 1970s–80s

LSI Game Invader 1000 with box, Gakken, 1980s

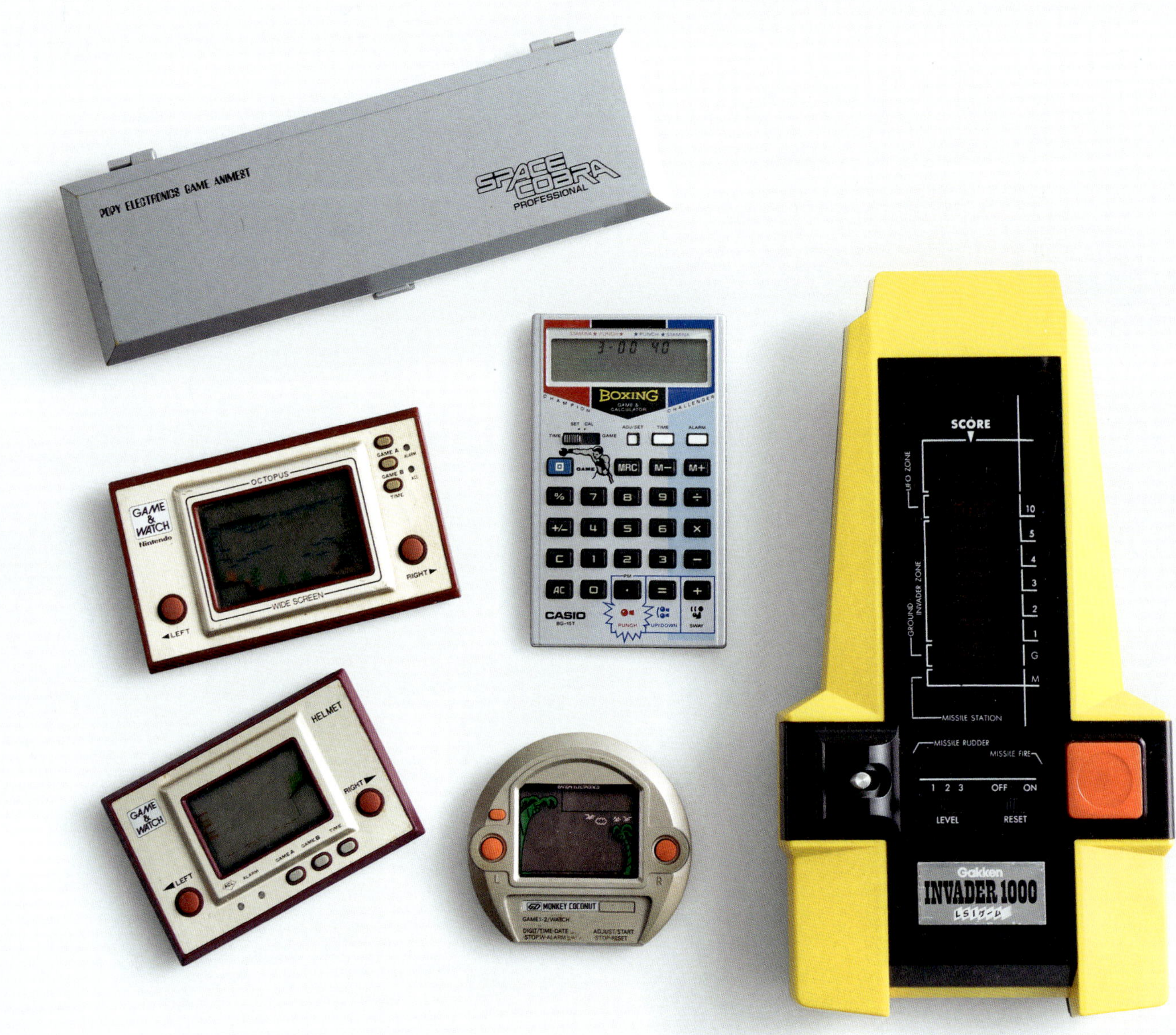

Car-shaped erasers, Iwako, 1980s

The Supercar Trading Cards, 1970s

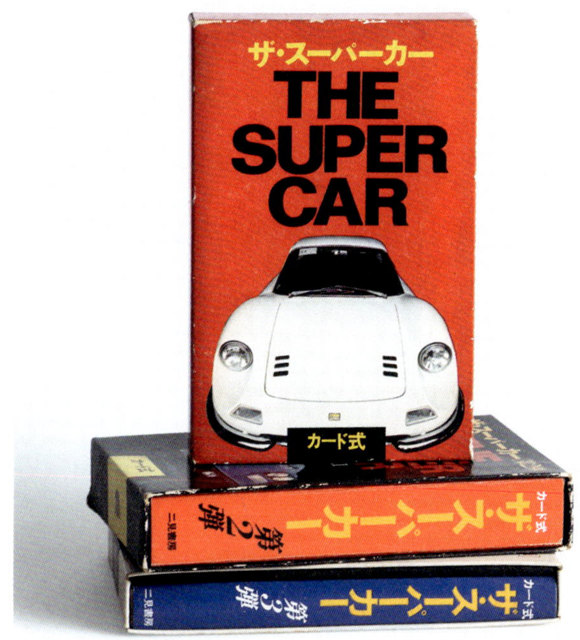

'This is actually a fake Rubik's Cube because I couldn't buy a real one.'

Denjin Zaborger Karuta (traditional Japanese playing cards), 1970s

The Game of Life board game, Milton Bradley, 1970s

GAME OF
F
E
ーム
I HEARTILY ENDORSE THIS GAME
Art Linkletter
TAKARA'S AMERICAN GAME
人生ゲーム
人生の波乱を繰りひろげながら早く億万長者になったひとが勝つゲームです
9才～成人向
家庭向
2～8人用
タカラのアメリカンゲームであそぼう
9才～成人向
家庭向
2～8 人用
人生ゲーム

Takeshi 'Beat' Kitano Lucky Cat coin bank, 1980s

Takeshi 'Beat' Kitano Lucky Cat T-shirt, 1980s

NIGO made these items as a child – the totem pole when he was six years old, and the *akabeko* (traditional Japanese folk toy, shaped like a red cow with a bobbing head) when he was in 3rd grade, class 5.

In kindergarten (aged four or five years old), NIGO played a cook in a school play – this was his pan. His mother wrote his name on it in white marker-pen. 'The white pens had become available in Japan around this time (there were only black pens before), which was such a cool thing.'

The first time that NIGO ever visited Tokyo (probably in 4th grade), he stayed at the luxury Hotel New Otani

Snoopy spoon, United Feature Syndicate, Inc, 1965

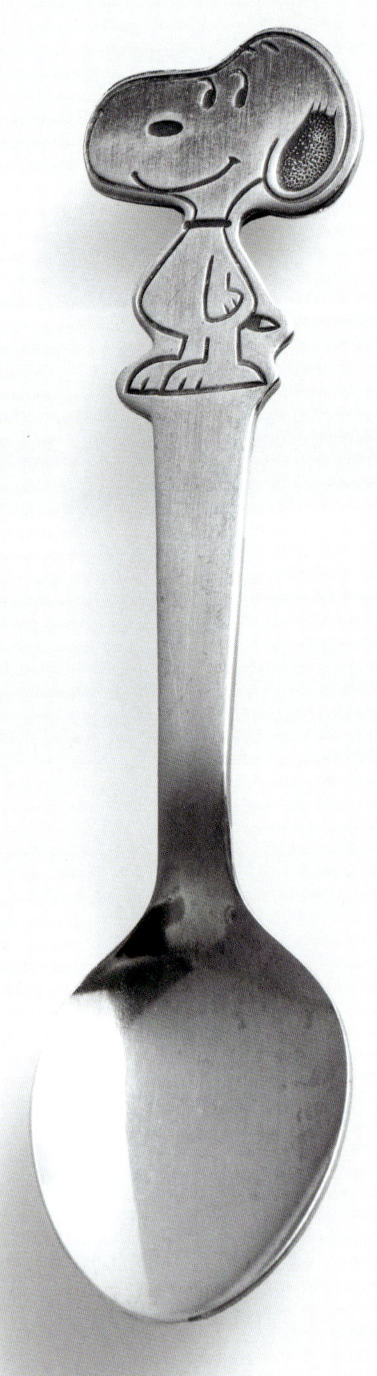

Star Wars Jawa figure with packaging, Kenner, 1977–1985. 'This is the first lot figure. People who bought it complained that the cape was made of vinyl and looked cheap, so from the second lot onwards the manufacturer changed the material to cloth – making the first lot a very rare Vinyl Cape Jawa.'

Tabletop baseball game, 1980s

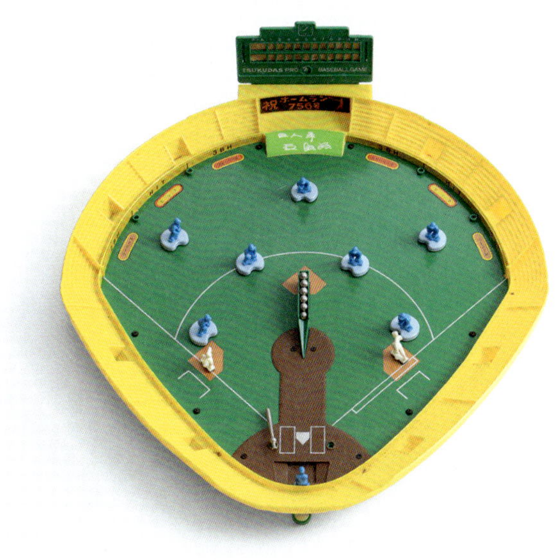

Model kit, Gundam, 1980s

Manga comic books. On top is *The Kabocha Wine*, which NIGO read in the 1980s. Below are books from the 1970s and 80s.

Yuusha Raideen jumbo figure in box, 1980s

Connecting human-shaped toys, PIKOTAN, 1970s. ‘These were promotional gifts that came with a Meiji company snack.’

Radio-controlled truck, owned by NIGO from 1st grade. ‘It only moves forward. My brother owned a radio-controlled Lamborghini. When the truck got stuck against a wall, I had to physically move it, but my brother could just back up his car.’

This was NIGO's favourite toy when he was a child. 'I used to play with it for four to five hours at a time.'

Car repair garage toy in box, 1970s

Electric pencil sharpener, pencils and pencil case, 1970s

Coupy-pencil set, Sakura, 1970s

'Origami *shuriken* (Ninja's hand-blade) that I folded myself. I loved folding origami, and made many different things.'

Russell Coca-Cola yo-yos, 1979. The accompanying pamphlets show the user how to master tricks. NIGO was a regional yo-yo champion.

INSIGHT

Pharell Williams and NIGO at a preview of their
Billionaire Boys Club and ICECREAM store in New York City, 2007

Pharrell Williams

'One of the greatest things we can witness as human beings is metamorphosis – change and growth. We see it in butterflies as they move from caterpillar to cocoon to flight. We see it in nature itself: in lakes, ponds, rivers, streams and oceans; as water evaporates, gathers in the clouds, builds pressure and weight, and eventually returns to us as rain.

This is NIGO-san.

I have watched him transform. I've seen him endure the roller-coasters of life – the highs and the lows – and still emerge on top. What he has accomplished in such a short span of time should truly be studied. He is my brother, and I look up to him not only as family, but as my teacher.

In time, those who don't yet understand will come to see. But for those of us who do, we continue to marvel at his constant evolution – his relentless metamorphosis. He only grows larger. He only shines brighter.

I've told him this many times: at every turning point, every moment of transformation, every transmutation into something new, more elevated, more refined – I say, this is your time. This is your year. And yet I find myself saying it again and again, because he never stops becoming.

Thank you, NIGO-san.
NIGO-sama – the highest honorific I can offer.
He was NIGO-san.
Now, he is NIGO-sama.'

NIGO first met Pharrell Williams through the New York jewellery designer Jacob the Jeweler. In the early 2000s NIGO commissioned Jacob to make pieces inspired by his vintage collection, such as the diamond-encrusted keychain illustrated on page 138. NIGO also asked Jacob to re-make pieces that he had seen Pharrell wearing. Struck by the pair's similar taste, Jacob arranged for NIGO and Pharrell to meet. This sparked a decades-long friendship and creative partnership. Recent collaboration includes the Louis Vuitton Men's Autumn/ Winter 2025 collection. Showcased in Paris, the collection was a celebration of their friendship, featuring 'Phriendship' graphics and influenced by a personal fishing trip.

In earlier days, when BAPE was increasing its presence on the global stage, Pharrell's group The Neptunes began playing at BAPE events, including the tenth anniversary party in 2003. In the same year, NIGO and Pharrell launched their joint fashion label, Billionaire Boys Club, debuting its designs in the music video for Pharrell's single 'Frontin''. Drawing heavily on skate culture, the label offered casual menswear classics such as jackets, sweaters and denim, all manufactured in Japan. The following year, they added a sneaker line, ICECREAM. Inspired by NIGO's love of classic American advertising, its shoeboxes were designed to look like ice cream tubs. A flagship store for both brands opened in Tokyo in 2005.

Beyond fashion, NIGO and Pharrell's work together includes serving as creative advisors and investors in the Japanese hospitality start-up NOT A HOTEL. In all their undertakings, their collaboration blends NIGO's take on Japanese culture with Pharrell's high-fashion, hip-hop influenced aesthetic. **Rosa Abbott**

HUMAN MADE seasonal lookbook, 2026

A BATHING APE

Evolution

Tiffany Godoy

NIGO's story is usually told backwards, as destiny. In real time, it was neither clean nor obvious. What emerged in Tokyo during the 1990s was a set of decisions made at close range, by people watching the same references and moving in step. It wasn't yet a movement. It was a code, and it circulated before it had a name.

When I arrived in Japan in 1997, streetwear was already everywhere, not as hype or product saturation, but as atmosphere. You felt it in magazines stacked at convenience stores, in record shops, in clubs and on the street. It functioned as a language. If you spoke it, you immediately knew who else did.

The backdrop matters. Japanese men's fashion was still processing the afterimage of the 1980s and the DC (designers and characters) brand boom. Brands such as MEN'S BIGI and others, inspired by Italian and French luxury, featured power shoulders, double-breasted jackets, glossy editorial fantasies. While designers such as Comme des Garçons and Yohji Yamamoto existed, of course, the socially dominant mood remained bubble-era: moneyed, performative, and increasingly disconnected from everyday reality.

The very first sketch by Sk8thing for a BAPE logo.

American casual and vintage culture followed, distinct from the California lifestyle romanticised by *Popeye* or Ivy League fantasies. This was *Shibukaji*: denim, workwear, military pieces – real clothes – filtered through Shibuya importers and early vintage. The approach was sincere but literal, too faithful to American bodies and context. What followed wasn't rejection. It was editing.

Ura-Harajuku became the site of that edit. Less a location than a method. NOWHERE, opening in 1993, operated as a filter rather than a shop, aligning undercover, imported references, and emerging with original work in a shared frame. Around it

United by a love of music and fashion, NIGO and Jun Takahashi wrote a column in *Takarajima*. Initially titled 'A–Z', it was soon renamed 'Last Orgy 2' in homage to Hiroshi Fujiwara and Kan Takagi's earlier column in the same magazine. Like its predecessor, it shared cult fashion items, DJ gear and pop culture, mixing punk and hip-hop influences. In 1993, they used it to announce the opening of the NOWHERE shop.

formed a tight constellation: Jun Takahashi, NIGO, Hiroshi Fujiwara, Kan Takagi of Major Force, Sk8thing, and a handful of others. They created primarily for each other, with limited releases circulating outward. No manifesto. Just instinct.

Both Jun and NIGO had come through Bunka Fashion College. That detail matters. The ambition wasn't to opt out of fashion, but to enter it properly, to build brands, to operate inside the system and bend it. That intent separated this moment from earlier subcultures which stayed deliberately outside.

The lineage starts earlier than most timelines admit. In 1987 Hiroshi Fujiwara and Kan Takagi's Tinnie Punx Last Orgy column in *Takarajima* magazine sparked a frenzy with its mix of street art, skate, club tracks and insider selections. Last Orgy became required reading, and by 1992 NIGO and Jun Takahashi carried the torch with their own column, Last Orgy 2 (and from 1995, Last Orgy 3). Even the name signalled allegiance.

Magazines were the connective tissue. Before the internet flattened everything, titles such as *smart*, *Boon*, *Asayan*, *Ollie*, *Relax* and *Warp* didn't simply report on culture. They constructed it. Serial columns created continuity and anticipation. You didn't scroll. You waited. And when you read, you recalibrated your eye. And then tried to get your hands on those limited-edition products.

NIGO stood out, not because he dominated the room but because he didn't. His public presence was famously controlled: poker-faced, neutral. A Japanese Warhol sample. He didn't narrate BAPE. He let it circulate. Graphics did the work. Camouflage, logos and characters developed with Sk8thing functioning as visual shorthand. When NIGO re-launched NOWHERE, Wonderwall reimagined it to include BAPE Gallery,

NIGO, *Ape Sounds*, Mo' Wax release in 2000.

showing Futura, Stash and later KAWS – all folded directly into product with highly collectable packaging. The T-shirts became a moving gallery.

Wearing BAPE wasn't about self-expression. It was about recognition. Tetsuya Suzuki, then editor-in-chief of *smart*, called it a 'password'. He was right. You didn't need to explain. The clothes already said enough.

At the same time, music was far more than an influence. It was infrastructure. DJs, electronic music, hip-hop (Fujiwara may have been the first to spin hip-hop in Japanese clubs) and remix culture all ran on the same logic. Sampling wasn't a trend, it was a world view. With the arrival of Photoshop, editing became democratic: take what exists, twist it, and make it yours. Fashion followed the same rules. Or – as its often summed up in relation to NIGO – first a collector, then a maker.

By the late 1990s, fashion and music were fully locked together for the brand. The Worldwide Ape Heads Shows at Akasaka Blitz in 1997 and Liquid Room in 1998 made that explicit, bringing together Japanese musician Cornelius, Japanese rapper Scha Dara Parr, US music producer Money Mark and British band Unkle. These weren't side projects. They were statements. In 1998, NIGO founded Ape Sounds, formalising music as part of the brand's DNA. The *Ape Sounds* album, released in 1999 and later internationally through Mo' Wax, sounded exactly like the world it came from.

Expansion followed sideways, rather than upward. Collaborations with Stüssy signalled peer recognition. BAPExclusive refined controlled access. Connections with Supreme deepened. Foot Soldier opened in Daikanyama. The BAPE STA sneaker entered the visual vocabulary.

International visibility arrived causally. Friends remember Cornelius wearing BAPE during his Point tour. In Paris, the influential boutique Colette placed it in the same sphere as Prada, treating it not as streetwear novelty but as another kind of mode. In a feat of reverse engineering to the US, NIGO's revered hip-hop scene provided the bridge. Images of the Beastie Boys wearing BAPE in 1999 circulated. The translation worked because the proposition was clear. All of this unfolds alongside major shifts in luxury itself. John Galliano landed at Dior in 1997. Marc Jacobs launched Louis Vuitton's first ready-to-wear collection the same year. Tom Ford rebuilt Gucci by 2000. Fashion was becoming personality driven, media aware and culturally legible. Street and luxury were no longer sealed off from one another.

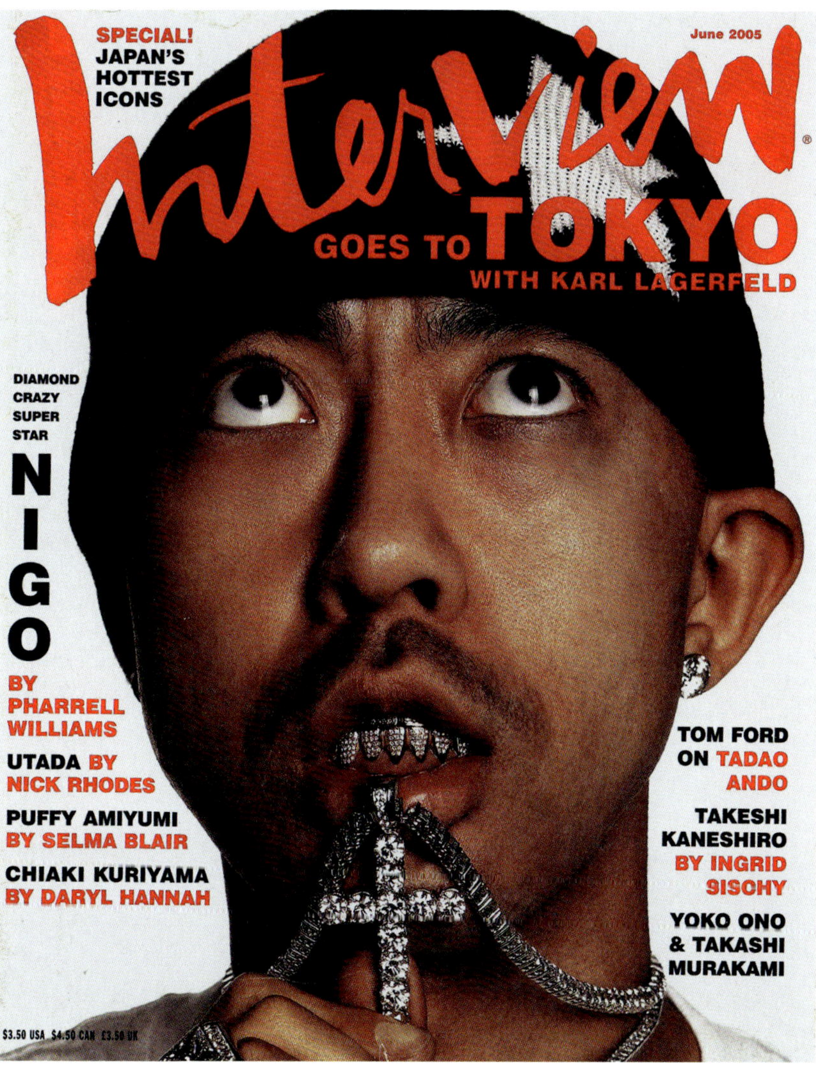

NIGO on the cover of *Interview* magazine, June 2005. Photography by Karl Lagerfeld, cover story interview conducted by Pharrell Williams. This issue focused on his work with A Bathing Ape (BAPE).

By the early 2000s, streetwear was no longer operating at the margins. Media projects such as BAPE TV expanded the universe. Tech collaborations followed. Baby Milo introduced a lighter, character-driven register. The Pepsi collaboration marked a visible shift – NIGO became a public figure. Crucially, he didn't resist this transition. He moved towards scale and visibility with intention. A decade after NOWHERE opened, the anniversary at WOMB with The Neptunes felt less like a celebration than confirmation.

By June 2005, the arc was impossible to miss. I was on set for *Interview* magazine's Tokyo issue as NIGO landed on the cover, photographed by Karl Lagerfeld, who had converted a floor of Chanel's Ginza boutique into a studio. Chrome Hearts rings helped to click the shutter as Karl clocked NIGO's diamond veneers and zoomed in. What began in the backstreets of Harajuku was now unmistakably global.

And yet the logic never disappeared. Around the same time, ICECREAM, launched with Pharrell Williams, operated directly opposite my Harajuku apartment. Its wi-fi signal appeared daily. Yoon from Ambush handled the PR. The scale had shifted, but the method had not.

Between 1993 and the early 2000s, the Ura-Hara scene and NIGO built the foundational system first. The industry then followed.

Photo of young NIGO with Hiroshi Fujiwara, 1989.

The Ura-Hara scene fused punk and hip-hop influences, and the band Tinnie Punx exemplified this. Formed by Hiroshi Fujiwara and Kan Takagi, Tinnie Punx combined Japanese rap with samples of American funk and British ska. Fujiwara and Takagi also wrote a column, 'Last Orgy', for the youth culture magazine *Takarajima*, reporting on music, DJing, skate culture, film and fashion.

Seiko Ito and Tinnie Punx, *Kensetsu-teki*.
Debut album, 21 September 1986

Teenage NIGO hung onto every word of Hiroshi Fujiwara's 'Last Orgy' column, which fed his appetite for hip-hop culture. He went to see Tinnie Punx DJ in his hometown of Maebashi in 1987, and asked them to sign his baseball cap and T-shirt.

When NIGO moved to Tokyo, he became Hiroshi Fujiwara's friend and assistant. His resemblance to Hiroshi earned him the nickname 'NIGO' (meaning 'number two' in Japanese), which was also shortened to '2GO'. This Montblanc pen was a gift from Fujiwara to NIGO, who was aspiring to be a fashion editor at the time.

NIGO began DJing at club nights in Tokyo in the late 1980s, including Family with Hiroshi Fujiwara

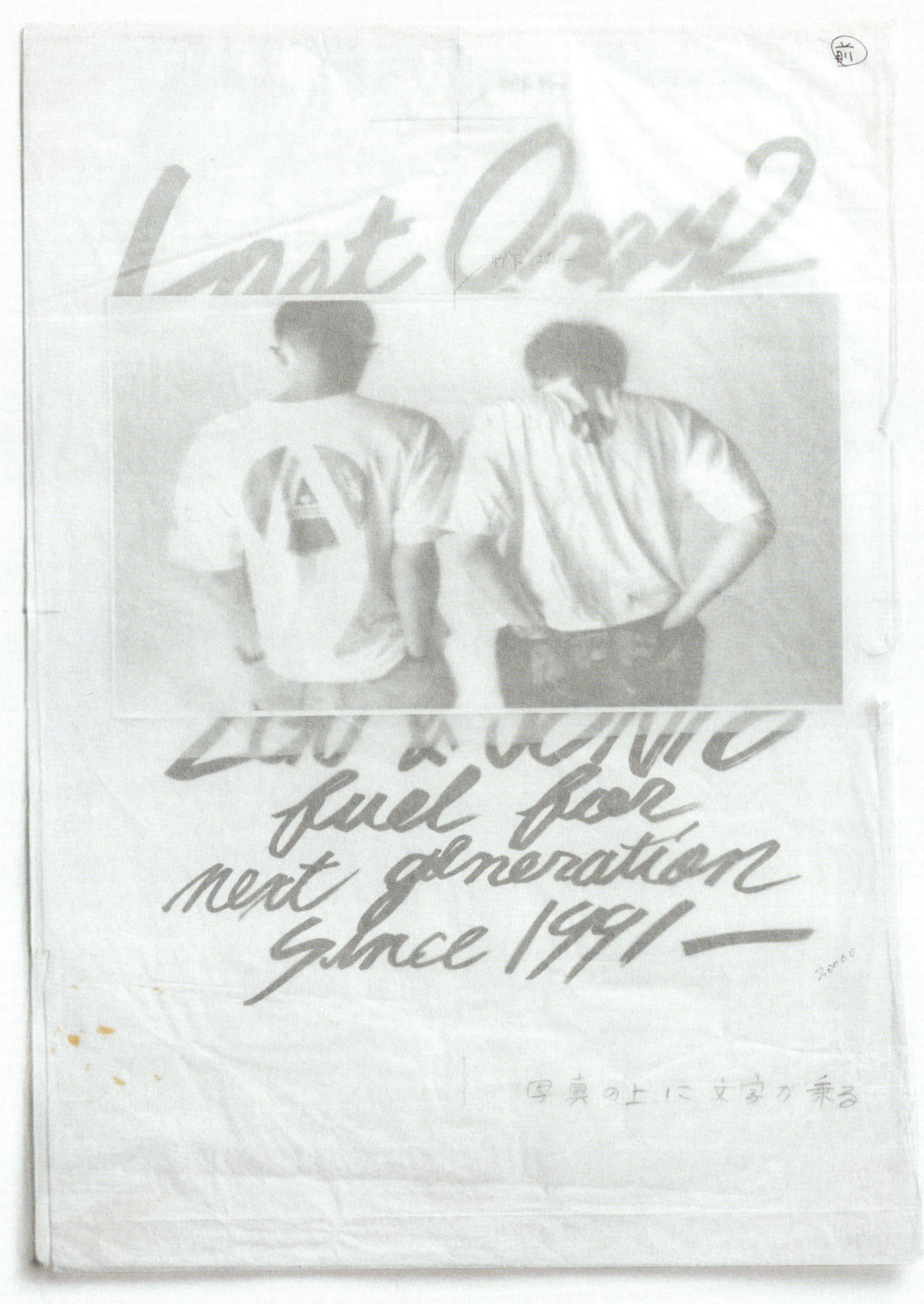
Last Orgy 2
fuel for
next generation
since 1991—
写真の上に文字が乗る

NIGO and Jun Takahashi wrote a column together and named it Last Orgy 2, in homage to Last Orgy. Through its pages, they also sold clothing and accessories, including varsity jackets, T-shirts and windbreakers. ‘The left page here shows the tech pack I assembled by hand, since no digital files existed at the time.’

Last Orgy 2 T-shirt

Last Orgy 2 sweatshirt

Last Orgy 2 nylon jacket

Last Orgy 2 varsity jacket

NOWHERE store signboard from 1993

Cardboard boxes used at NOWHERE

The first shopping bag designed for NOWHERE

The second shopping bag designed for NOWHERE

NOWHERE 3rd anniversary collectible set

This T-shirt is known by collectors as the A-Bomb T-shirt', 1993. It features a graphic by Sk8thing and a 'Boombox tag', seen only on the earliest designs.

'These were the second jeans we made at BAPE. I liked the Levi's 505 silhouette which is slightly skinny with big pockets, hence this design.'

Early BAPE designs, printed on Camber sweatshirts and featuring the 'Boombox tag'

A BATHING APE
GENERALS

BAPE early era nylon jacket. 'This was the very first item that was published in *The Face* magazine. US graffiti artist Futura was wearing this jacket, that he bought in London, when I first met him in Tokyo.'

Early BAPE varsity jacket

'I made this collaboration Cowchin with POST O'ALLS, in Canada.'

The very first BAPE Camo item

Hip-hop icon Biggie Smalls, also known as The Notorious B.I.G, catapulted the BAPE camo print to global fame. Custom XXL pieces were created for the rapper, but unfortunately they did not reach him before his untimely death in 1997.

Ape Map of Harajuku, 1996. The mid-1990s saw A Bathing Ape expand, opening new stores in Tokyo including 'secret' shops, which were discreetly illustrated on this 'Ape map'.

'This is the invitation of the very first exhibition I did. When you open it, there are film slides. Included in the box is a viewer so that you can look at the slides.'

BAPE camo print pencils

Compressed T-shirts in tins inspired by spray cans – collaboration with American street artists Stash and Futura, 1997

In 2001 NIGO approached Pepsi to collaborate on limited-edition BAPE merchandise. This collaboration paved the way for future high-profile fashion-corporate partnerships. NIGO's vision was to release Pepsi cans plastered with his iconic camo pattern, bringing BAPE to a wider consumer base. These cans retailed for less than a dollar, making them the most affordable BAPE item at the time. They became instant collector's items and have since become highly sought-after by a community of hard-core BAPE fans.

T-shirt from the 2002 collaboration with New York skateboarding brand Supreme, reflecting BAPE's increasing international reach in this era

In 2005, BAPE collaborated with cosmetics brand MAC on a line of products including washbags, lip conditioner and blotting film. They all feature BAPE's distinctive camo print

This Nintendo DS Lite (2008) was decorated with graphics of BAPE's Baby Milo character alongside Mario

The BAPE STA is one of the brand's most iconic products. Modelled on Nike's Air Force 1, a classic 1980s basketball shoe, the design replaces Nike's 'swoosh' with a shooting star motif. Limited editions, luxury materials and collaborations elevated the shoe to a luxury object and collector's item. 'Chompers', with their playful tooth graphics, are one of NIGO's many collaborations with the artist KAWS.

APL

Zukka Baby Milo Bag Charm, a collaboration between BAPE and Fendi. To celebrate the collaboration, a party was held at one of the Olympic venues in Harajuku. A young Virgil Abloh was among the guests, and NIGO introduced him to Michael Burke, then CEO of Fendi. Burke later went on to manage the Louis Vuitton brand and hired Virgil as the creative director.

Baby Milo T-shirt, Baby Milo and Chrome Hearts, 2009. Created in 1999, Baby Milo was based on a character from the 1971 film *Escape from Planet of the Apes* and influenced by Sanrio. Illustrated in a kid-friendly blocky style, the mascot has been emblazoned on everything from T-shirts to accessories and soft toys.

Diamond keychain, early 2000s. NIGO commissioned New York designer Jacob the Jeweler to create this piece, inspired by an item from his vintage collection. Jacob also introduced NIGO and Pharrell Williams, sparking a decades-long friendship and creative partnership.

Diamond veneers, 2017. Dental jewellery was popularised by Black American rap artists in the 1990s, symbolising status and self-expression. NIGO began wearing them at a time in which his design aesthetic and collaborations were deeply embedded within the hip-hop community. Unlike grillz, which are removable, NIGO opted for diamond veneers, a more permanent procedure in which jewellery is bonded directly to teeth.

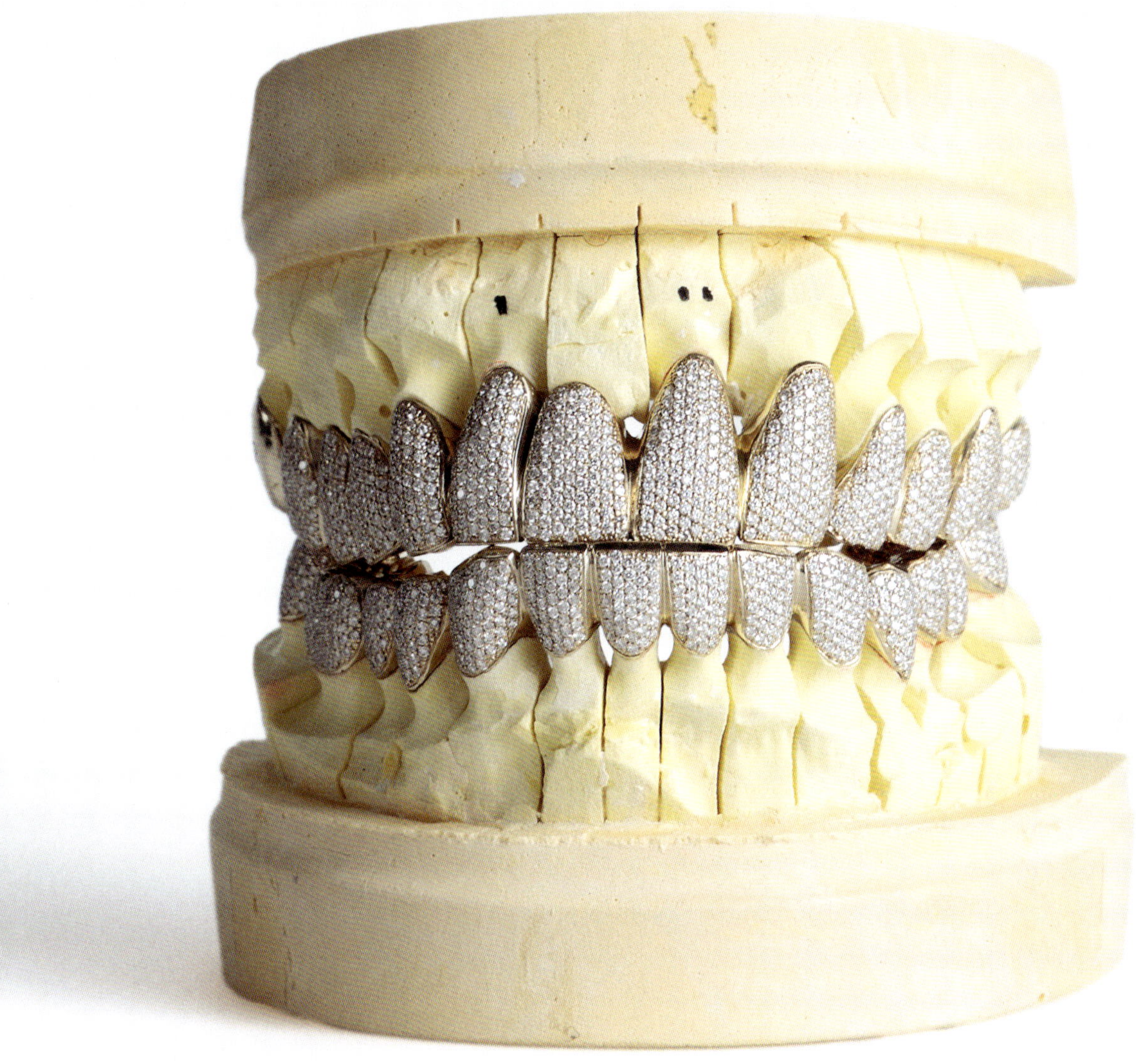

From 2002 NIGO partnered with All Japan Pro Wrestling on wrestling events. Contestants entered a BAPE camo ring, wearing BAPE T-shirts to the sound of NIGO's music. Wrestlers would also make one-off appearances as characters from NIGO's universe, such as the monkey-themed Super Milo, whose mask is among those pictured here.

NIGO used his retail spaces to champion his favourite artists. These action figurines – representing Futura, NIGO and Mo' Wax Records founder James Lavelle – were launched at Stash and Futura's COMMAND-Z exhibition at NOWHERE in 2000.

NIGO created the Mr. Bathing Ape tailoring line in 2011 for BAPE's loyal customers in search of a more mature look. These hybrids of a brogue shoe by Regal and BAPE STA trainer, from 2012, capture NIGO's approach to the 'formal Western wardrobe'.

NIGO established record label Ape Sounds and released his first album in the late 1990s. In 2004 he created hip-hop supergroup Teriyaki Boyz. They worked with leading rappers and producers, such as Daft Punk, The Neptunes and DJ Premiere. Their soundtrack for *The Fast and the Furious: Tokyo Drift* has charted in the top ten most-streamed songs by Japanese artists overseas for twenty years. He also produced pop-punk girl group Billie Idle, with their playful subversion of Japanese 'pop idol' culture with the slogan 'NOT IDOLS'.

Plastic food models *(shokuhin sampuru)* are commonplace in Japan, and considered a craft. This hyperrealistic chicken burger model was released to promote Teriyaki Boyz's first album *Beef or Chicken* in 2005.

KAWS, *The Death of NIGO*, 2004. In 2013 NIGO stepped down from A Bathing Ape after twenty years leading the brand. He announced his departure in a blog post, sharing an image of this painting with the caption 'BAPE GENERAL NIGO® (1993–2013)'. It is said that the first Tokugawa shōgun, Ieyasu (1543–1616), commissioned a portrait of himself after suffering his greatest military defeat. He carried it around to remind himself not to commit the same mistakes. NIGO states that this painting acts in a similar way for him, encouraging self-reflection and personal growth.

'I designed the blister-pack frame to display KAWS' paintings. He gifted this one to me. I keep it close as a reminder to never make the same mistake again.'

In 2003 NIGO and Pharrell Williams launched their fashion label, Billionaire Boys Club. Drawing on skate culture, the label offers casual menswear classics like jackets, sweaters and denim, all manufactured in Japan.

A year after launching Billionaire Boys Club, NIGO and Pharrell added a sneaker line, ICECREAM. Inspired by NIGO's love of classic American advertising, its shoeboxes were designed to look like ice cream tubs.

One of the first pieces NIGO designed for HUMAN MADE, this jacket takes inspiration from his collection of vintage *sukajan* jackets. He kept the flight jacket-inspired silhouette, but gave the classic animal motifs a futuristic refashioning, with bears stylised as rocket ships. The embroidery applied over printed designs creates more depth and texture.

As with many original *sukajan*, the design of the jacket shown opposite is reversible.

Lubbock High School yearbook, 1955. Taking pride of place in NIGO's archive is this graduation yearbook signed by music icon Buddy Holly (born Charles Hardin Holley). The singer's autograph appears next to a photo of his eighteen-year-old self.

'Charlie' mannequin, 2010–22. This mannequin was inspired by Buddy Holly from the year book album on the left and by 1950s shop dummies. The mannequin and glasses were subsequently used to display NIGO's vintage collection at the Bunka Gakuen Costume Museum in 2022.

Mr. Peanut *tsuriami* sweatshirt, HUMAN MADE, 2025 – NIGO's homage to the sweatshirt on page 78. Mr. Peanut is the mascot for American snack brand Planters. The sweatshirt is an example of *tsuriami* knitting, which uses a slow, low-tension loop wheel knitting machine to create a plush and bouncy texture with a soft and airy feel.

Mr. Peanut *hariko* figure, HUMAN MADE, 2025

Crates, HUMAN MADE, 2020s. 'This is one of the most popular, iconic HUMAN MADE items. It always sells out on the first day.'

In 2019 NIGO and Pharrell Williams launched Storm Cowboy sake. Made at Ohmine Shuzou, a boutique sake brewery combining a modern outlook with traditional techniques, it features an eye-catching graphic and is available in light, middle, heavy and natural pressings. Storm Cowboy won a gold medal at the prestigious International Wine Challenge (IWC) in 2020.

NIGO has developed HUMAN MADE lifestyle products that recreate highly collectible pieces of early 20th-century Americana using traditional Japanese techniques. Handmade in Japan, these figures combine vintage American advertising with Japan's long history of crafting papier-mâché figures (*hariko*) as good luck charms. These hariko ducks reference NIGO's collection of 1920s wooden hunting ducks.

STRM
DRYALLs
CWBY
HUMAN
MADE
®

INSIGHT

Promotional photo of TET and NIGO for the DOUBTFUL AS DOUBLE marketing campaign, 2014

TET Nishiyama

'The time was the late 1980s. It was when Japan's bubble economy was at its peak. I believe the first time we met was at HF's house [Hiroshi Fujiwara]. If my memory is correct, that was also the day he was given the name "NIGO".

More than thirty years have passed since then, bringing us to the present. This exhibition is also an opportunity to look back on the past three decades. As someone who has spent much of that time alongside him, I tried to reflect on the figure of NIGO from my own perspective. Of course, he himself might reject this way of looking at things. So I hope it will simply be received as a personal view.

The world we inhabit is one where new things are constantly appearing and disappearing. You could even say it is a world where chasing trends itself is considered "the latest." Yet within that environment, NIGO has carefully picked up fragments of past events and cultures that many people overlook. And by patiently connecting those pieces together, he has continued to give them form as something new.

What emerges from this process is slightly different from what we usually call trends or the latest thing. Within the current of inspiration that he has accumulated over a long period of time, many different elements flow together and are thoughtfully presented to the world with a clear sense of context.

NIGO's interests and actions are always connected – point to point. And that line never breaks.

He gathers fragments from the past and passes them on to the future. To do this, he engages with an immense archive more deeply than almost anyone else. And through a remarkable editorial sensibility, he presents them again as new value.

NIGO is not someone who looks back at the past with nostalgia. Rather, he is someone who carries fragments of the past forward into the future.'

Tetsu Nishiyama, also known as TET, is a creative director and streetwear pioneer. He was a member of the Ura-Hara scene formed in Harajuku in the early 1990s.

TET launched his first brand, FPAR (Forty Percent Against Rights), with friends in 1993. He used silkscreen printing to emblazon T-shirts and other simple garments with provocative slogans and graphics. Like NIGO and other peers at the time, TET drew inspiration from foreign fanzines, magazines and pop culture. In 1996 he followed up with a second brand, WTAPS, celebrated for its military details, high-performance materials and utilitarian style. Even the name was a military reference – pronounced 'double taps', it refers to two bullets fired in rapid succession at the same target (FPAR being the first 'shot').

TET and NIGO have frequently collaborated over the decades – starting in 1993, when NOWHERE became an early stockist of FPAR. Their partnership has since encompassed official brand ventures, mutual artistic projects and personal support, often blending Nishiyama's utilitarian, military-inspired aesthetic with NIGO's pop culture-driven style. This includes DOUBTFUL AS DOUBLE® (2014–15), a joint venture deeply influenced by 1980s Japanese pop culture, hip-hop and DJs. HUMAN MADE and WTAPS collaborated in 2019.

In April 2026 TET was appointed creative director of Buffer, a new label by HUMAN MADE. With a pink rabbit as its mascot the brand seeks to connect generations, drawing upon American pop culture and Tokyo youth culture from the 1980s, 1990s and 2000s. **Rosa Abbott**

Sauce sachets, Curry Up, 2010s. The logo for NIGO's restaurant, Curry Up, was designed by TET. Offering a mix of Japanese and Indian curries, the recipes and design style were inspired by NIGO's student job at a small but popular Indian eatery called Ghee.

NIGO

The NIGO Effect

Rachel Hajek and Esme Hawes

'Prior to pop-culture embracing the niche, the marginal and the street, NIGO was already curating a realm of prominent artists to expose that which was combusting beneath the surface', said designer and artist Virgil Abloh in 2020, two years into his position as artistic director of menswear at Louis Vuitton. Abloh saw himself as a descendent of this new way of thinking, one which valued artforms outside of traditional institutions and built a bridge connecting the two. This is NIGO's legacy, built over three decades of practice.

Queue outside BAPE, London, 2002.

Today, it is nothing out of the ordinary to see scores of people queuing outside storefronts waiting for the latest release, paying upwards of triple figures for a T-shirt or sneakers, and creative directors of fashion houses who are not just designers but public figures. Neither are collaborations between brands and individual designers or artists, 'drops' and limited-edition releases, the idea of 'influence' itself, even. So entrenched are these practices within the realm of fashion retail, it is easy to forget they are a relatively recent phenomena. They have, in fact, only become part of mainstream retail culture within the last few decades, and NIGO was a prominent flagbearer for these trends.

Some thirty years ago, before widespread use of the internet, let alone the dawn of social media, what is described above could only be found in small corners of the world, among pockets of youth culture, divulged through magazine spreads and word of mouth.

In the backstreets of Harajuku, Tokyo, an approach to design that NIGO and his peers was pioneering in the 1990s was to have a huge impact on consumers and designers alike, the legacy of which is still felt today. It's a phenomenon dubbed the 'NIGO effect'.

When starting up his label A Bathing Ape, NIGO inadvertently paved the way for much of youth and fashion culture that followed. Starting up with limited resources, early BAPE products were produced in limited stock (only five of each product!). He referenced and sampled from the popular culture he grew up with and obsessed over. The close-knit community of designers, artists, musicians and magazine editors to which he belonged frequently worked together. He paid as much detail to creating the experience of encountering his designs as he did to the designs themselves.

What resulted were highly covetable items, a dedicated fanbase and community built around shared interests, and a revised understanding of what counts as luxury. Suddenly, staple garments such as T-shirts and merchandise in the form of everyday objects became collectors' items, a signal to others that the owner was part of the cognoscenti. 'High' and 'low' mixed seamlessly, taking the formality out of the former and putting the latter on a pedestal. NIGO's designs and the worlds built around them amassed a cult following, whose members would go to great lengths to own these fragments of his worldview. To this day, they hold on to unopened cans of Pepsi wrapped in BAPE's signature camo print, flyers from NIGO's branded events, limited-edition shopping bags, shoe boxes and ephemera gifted to the most dedicated of fans. The meteoric success of the brand, and the level of dedication its followers demonstrated, was something that countless competitors attempted to replicate. It has made NIGO and the brands he has created part of popular culture, from mentions in song lyrics (examples include Soulja Boy's 'Bapes' and Stormzy's 'NIGO Duppy') to appearing in

Foot Soldier, 2001.

BAPE STORE® Los Angeles, 2008.

contemporary artists' works – most recently Henry James's portrait of Pharrell Williams wearing a HUMAN MADE cap, which featured on the cover of *Vogue*.

With his track record NIGO cemented his reputation as a global tastemaker. His eye for the new, the unexpected, the eclectic, and his careful selection of partnerships, has consistently appealed to wide and global audiences. Such was the value and power of his all-encompassing vision that he himself became a sought-after collaborator, surpassing the brands he had been at the helm of. NIGO became the first ever creative director for Uniqlo's UT line in 2014. and designed the 2022 World Cup strip for the Japanese team in collaboration with adidas. In 2024, following a historically challenging relationship due to the Bapesta's resemblance to the Airforce I trainer, NIGO was invited by Nike to design a series of exclusive Air Force III sneakers and clothing collections. From one-off products and capsule collections to creative direction, to be associated with NIGO is to be current.

Few creative figures have put their names to such a breadth of partners as NIGO, demonstrating not only the reach of his appeal but also the astonishing range of inspiration NIGO draws from, from streetwear and sportswear brands to European luxury fashion houses. NIGO was appointed artistic director of KENZO in 2021, the first Japanese designer since Kenzō Takada himself. While fashion houses have adopted 'street' aesthetics before, this appointment showcased a move towards employing a key trendsetter, giving NIGO a top seat at the table of high fashion. His debut collection was a masterclass in reworking archival material, showing a deep respect for the fashion house's signature codes. As is key in all of

Louis Vuitton Cotteville, from the 2020 Louis Vuitton and NIGO capsule collaboration with Virgil Abloh. This limited edition of the familiar Louis Vuitton 1930s-inspired case is now highly collectable.

NIGO and Pharrell at the Louis Vuitton Menswear Autumn/Winter 2025 show.

NIGO's partnerships, there is a deep respect for and interest in the past, while always reinventing and creating something new. This move to high-end fashion culminated in a joint collection between NIGO and long-time friend and collaborator, Pharrell Williams, for Louis Vuitton's Men's line in January 2025.

However, it is not only brands that benefit from having 'NIGO ×' next to their names, but up-and-coming designers and artists too. Since the beginning of his career, an important part of NIGO's craft has been amplifying voices from the underground and the margins. In the 1990s, this took the form of New York street artists or Japanese hip-hop and *Shibuya-kei* stars. Over thirty years on, he is still using seats of influence and platforms to champion those who excite him, his eye as keen as ever to find voices that represent the youth culture of the present that shapes the mainstream today. The importance NIGO places on mentorship and patronage perhaps stems from his own experiences coming up as a young DJ and stylist, when he was taken under the wing of fashion, music and culture pioneer, Hiroshi Fujiwara. Once a student, NIGO is now a master. Practitioners whom he admires and chooses to work with are often propelled into his spotlight. Such is another strand of the almighty 'NIGO effect' – paving the way for others to follow in his path.

NIGOLD collection blazer, NIGO and UNITED ARROWS, 2015. Pharrell Williams wore this blazer at the Cannes Film Festival in 2015. Its print is based on an illustration by contemporary Japanese artist Eizin Suzuki, who is known for his bright and bold depictions of nostalgic American scenes.

'Charles' glasses, EFFECTOR by NIGO, 2010.
In 2010 NIGO created designs in tribute to 1950s musician Buddy Holly, collaborating with Japanese eyewear brand EFFECTOR. Heavily influenced by mid-century styles, the 'Charles' echoed the late musician's thick black frames, while the 'Holly' had a more casual style.

LV Made duck, Louis Vuitton by Virgil Abloh, in collaboration with NIGO, pre-collection Autumn/Winter 2020. As artistic director of Louis Vuitton menswear, Virgil Abloh called upon his ‘spiritual mentor’ NIGO in 2020 for a unique collaboration. The result was the LV^2 capsule clothing collection, which also included this ‘LV Made’ mallard duck, a nod to HUMAN MADE.

Snoopy plush toy, NIGO for Uniqlo and KAWS, 2017. As creative director of Uniqlo's UT Line, NIGO tapped into his extensive network, collaborating with long-time creative partner KAWS to reinterpret classic *Peanuts* and *Sesame Street* characters.

Snoopy UT T-shirt, NIGO for Uniqlo and KAWS, 2017

Sesame Street UT T-shirt, NIGO for Uniqlo and KAWS, 2017

Sesame Street stuffed toys, NIGO for Uniqlo and KAWS, 2017

Star Wars UT T-shirt, designed by NIGO for Uniqlo, 2019. Brought in by NIGO. Jun Takahashi and Tetsu Nishiyama also participated in this collaboration with their own designs featuring motifs from *Star Wars*.

Yoda backpack Uniqlo UT T-shirt. Designed by NIGO.

Front design of Yoda backpack Uniqlo UT T-shirt

In 2015 NIGO was approached by ABEMA, a new Japanese streaming service, to design their company logo. With the spread of smartphones, the company recognised that creative branding was required to compete and stand out. Keenly aware of the power of an eye-catching mascot, NIGO designed this animal character for ABEMA. He retained the green from the original logo, creating playful, dynamic branding that is immediately recognisable.

Japan National Team Special Collection kit, NIGO and adidas, 2022. Designed for the 2022 World Cup, this shirt is signed by the entire Japanese national football team. Its colours were inspired by *sakura mochi*, a traditional cherry blossom-coloured Japanese sweet wrapped in a cherry leaf.

T-shirt, Nike × NIGO, 2024

Sweatshirt, Nike × NIGO, 2024

Varsity jacket, Nike × NIGO, 2024.
Friends and family colour, not for sale.

NIGO

In 2025 NIGO brought Levi's on board for a collaboration with Nike, creating a denim version of their classic Air Force III low trainers. Featured in the advertising campaign was this life-size cut-out of NIGO as a denim-clad cowboy.

Hariko figure, HUMAN MADE and Keiko Sootome, 2025. Japanese illustrator Keiko Sootome's collaboration with HUMAN MADE features her signature playful figures painted with retro colours in her unique painterly style. The series also incorporates the Japanese *hariko* papier-mâché technique, used for centuries to create folk toys.

L–R

Louis Vuitton Men's Pre Collection Spring-Summer 2022, Look 6
Louis Vuitton Men's Pre Collection Autumn-Winter 2020, Look 8
Louis Vuitton Men's Autumn-Winter 2025 Show, Look 56

L–R

KENZO Autumn-Winter 2023, Look 1
KENZO Spring-Summer 2025, Look 21
KENZO Autumn-Winter 2022, Look 17

L–R

KENZO Autumn-Winter 2025, Look 17
KENZO Autumn-Winter 2025, Look 10
KENZO Autumn-Winter 2024, Look 53

INSIGHT

Fraser Cooke, Sacai Backstage,
Paris Men's Fashion Week, January 2026

Fraser Cooke

'*Amekaji* is really NIGO's thing ... He has got his archive really well documented. He'll be able to pull out a magazine and turn to a page and say this is the thing that inspired me when I was young. He's very organised – he's a nerd basically!'

'When Jun Takahashi and NIGO did *Last Orgy 2*, they were showing stuff they were interested in. They were travelling, picking stuff up. This was pre-internet. They were gatekeepers of information. The thing about NIGO is that he's a real expert in referencing archetypes or classics. If you look at early Bathing Ape, really it was re-making things that already existed that he thought were interesting and iconic classic items.'

'In my job at Nike I have worked with a lot of designers and creatives ... NIGO is very good at thinking about the overall picture. NIGO has an archival knowledge of all the classic things to draw upon. He's good with colour. He's quite fast and very organised, and has good people around him. He's not a fashion designer [in the traditional sense], but those people are not always as good at the last part, how you bring it to life. They're just good at making the thing. NIGO is good at repackaging things and giving an interesting spin. He has a good idea of what he wants to work on and why it's important to him, because he's not creating something out of nowhere. NIGO is a complete stylist. He is very hardworking and very committed. However, he doesn't ruminate on the details for ages; he's quite fast and quite focussed.'

Fraser Cooke, special projects senior director at Nike, has known NIGO as a friend and collaborator for the last thirty or so years. Cooke's enthusiasm for Japanese subculture magazines meant that he was aware of NIGO and the Ura-Hara scene when they met by chance during the mid-1990s. At this first encounter, on a London street, Cooke initially mistook NIGO for his mentor, Hiroshi Fujiwara (a mistake made by many). To cement their new friendship, NIGO gifted Cooke a hand-printed T-shirt, which turned out to be one of his very early BAPE creations.

At the time, Cooke was working with Michael Kopelman at Gimme Five, a London-based distributor of niche Japanese and American brands. In 1997 they opened Hideout in London's Soho, which became one of the first stores in the UK to stock and sell A Bathing Ape. As a result, Cooke made his first trip to Tokyo later that year, where he spent more time with NIGO. They soon discovered that they had a shared circle of friends within the burgeoning sub-cultural scenes of both London and Tokyo. Notably, Cooke shared a flat back in London with James Lavelle from Unkle, an early musical collaborator of NIGO's.

NIGO and Cooke crossed paths again in California, this time at the Action Sports Retailer trade show in San Diego. Attended by both American and Japanese retailers, this is where emerging sub-cultural skateboarding and surf brands started to show their collections in the late 1990s. It was during this time that they had a chance visit to *Planet of the Apes* actor Roddy McDowall's house in Los Angeles, to see one of the original statues used in the film.

Since starting at Nike in 2004, Cooke has been instrumental in some of the brand's most iconic collaborations, with designers including Kim Jones, Virgil Abloh, Ricardo Tiscci and Chitose Abe at Sacai. Since 2025 he has worked closely with NIGO on a series of exclusive Nike Air Force III sneakers and clothing collections. Through this collaboration, Cooke has commented on NIGO's keen focus on detail, in everything from the shoebox design to promotional imagery and associated merchandise to create a full experience of the product. Cooke also talks of his admiration for NIGO's encyclopaedic knowledge of cultural references which he brings to reimagining Nike's classic models. **Fiona McKay**

Fraser Cooke, Komazawa Olympic Park, Tokyo, summer 2025

New Traditions

Yuka Ryusenji

Chanoyu (the Japanese tea ceremony) is one of Japan's traditional cultural practices with a long history. In order for host and guest to share and enjoy a single bowl of tea, the host devotes careful thought to every utensil and every element used in the tea gathering, producing the tearoom as a complete environment. Its physical components span a wide range – architecture, calligraphy, painting, ceramics, lacquerware, bamboo crafts, dyed textiles, cuisine, sweets and matcha – each imbued with a uniquely Japanese aesthetic sensibility. *Sadō* (the Way of Tea) is a set of practices and rituals for preparing tea, infused with deep spirituality closely connected to Zen thought and a spirit of hospitality. *Chanoyu*, which encompasses all of these elements, is therefore often described as a comprehensive Japanese art form.

While NIGO is extremely busy with his primary work, he has also been immersed in the world of *chanoyu* for around the past decade. The initial impetus came largely from the influence of his wife, who had been pursuing tea practice ahead of him, but as his activities expanded onto the global stage it may also have been a result of his renewed recognition of the appeal of Japanese culture. With his characteristic diligence he studied *sadō* seriously, and gradually became absorbed in the depth of the world of *chanoyu*.

Among the many tea utensils, the *chawan* (tea bowl) – which the guest takes into their hands, brings to their lips, and from which they drink the tea – plays a particularly important role as an anchor through which the host's intentions and sensibility are conveyed to the guest. For NIGO, a creator by nature, it was a natural progression that his commitment to tea utensils would lead him to begin making tea bowls himself.

NIGO has travelled to kilns throughout Japan, seeking instruction from local ceramic artists and devoting himself to pottery-making in pursuit of his ideal tea bowl. The ceramic artists who guide NIGO, a novice in ceramics, are deeply moved by his humble and stoic approach to making tea bowls and do not hesitate to lend their support. At the same time, professional ceramic artists themselves are stimulated by NIGO's attitude towards creation. At present, NIGO's tea bowl practice involves earnestly learning and respecting the traditions and techniques cherished by each kiln, repeatedly training at the wheel, and gradually allowing his own distinct sensibility to emerge.

Speaking about ceramics, NIGO says: 'There has never been anything in my life that I have been this absorbed in, nor anything that refuses to turn out as I imagine it quite like this.' Unlike making clothing, the outcome must ultimately be entrusted to the action of the flames inside the kiln – that is, to the forces of nature. In addition to the interaction of clay, glaze and fire, timing in many forms is also crucial. After much trial and error, only a handful of works remain that truly satisfy him. It is precisely for this reason that his curiosity and spirit of challenge are continually stirred.

NIGO greatly admires Kawakita Handeishi (1878–1963). Handeishi was a banker who also gained renown as an amateur ceramic artist. NIGO is known as a major collector of Handeishi's works. From autumn 2025 to spring 2026, a special exhibition, *NIGO and Handeishi*, was held at two venues in Mie and Kyoto. The exhibition attracted many visitors who admire NIGO, including young people who had previously had little opportunity to encounter *chanoyu* or ceramics. All were captivated by the worlds of these two figures. The tea bowls of NIGO and Handeishi – and NIGO's works in particular – possess a persuasive power that requires no explanation.

NIGO hopes that his creative work can become 'a catalyst through which the wonderful Japanese cultures of ceramics and *sadō* are passed on to the next generation'. His ceramics, in which tradition and innovation merge, truly embody the phrase 'The Future is in the Past'. Through NIGO, the traditional Japanese cultures of *chanoyu* and ceramics are now beginning to resonate unmistakably in the hearts of young people around the world who will shape the next generation.

Shigaraki Warikoudai Tea Bowl (Takakura Kiln), 2025

'Iroe' glaze Tea Bowl (Senkaku Kiln), 2025

‘Haiyu’ glaze Tea Bowl (Sakakura Shinbei Kiln), 2025

Iga Shioge Tea Bowl (Takakura Kiln), 2024

Shigaraki Higakimon Tea Bowl (Takakura Kiln), 2025

Karatsu Tea Bowl (Tonoyama Kiln), 2025

Seiji Tea Bowl (Takakura Kiln), 2025

Irabo Tea Bowl (Futouan), 2023

Ido Warikoudai Tea Bowl (Futouan), 2023

Black Tea Bowl (Futouan), 2024

Karatsu Shioge Tea Bowl (Tonoyama Kiln), 2025

Hagi 'Haiyu' glaze Tea Bowl (Tahara Toubei Atelier), 2025

‘The glaze inside the tea bowl happened to shrink into a heart shape.’

Seal mark on the foot rim

Hagi Tea Bowl (Sakakura Shinbei Kiln), 2025

Shino Tea Bowl (Yuka Hayashi Atelier), 2025

Hagi Tea Bowl (Miwa Kiln), 2024

Ido Tea Bowl (Futouan), 2024

Hori Karatsu Tea Bowl (Tonoyama Kiln), 2025

Black Tea Bowl (Futouan), 2024

Hagi Kutsugata Tea Bowl (Sakakura Shinbei Kiln), 2023

Hagi Tea Bowl (Miwa Kiln), 2024

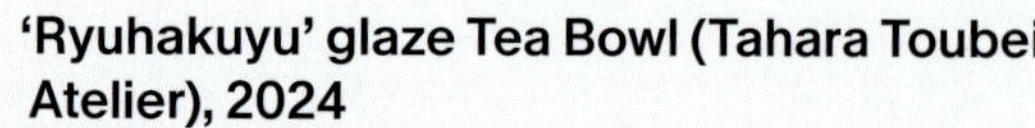

'Ryuhakuyu' glaze Tea Bowl (Tahara Toubei Atelier), 2024

Hagi Tea Bowl (Sakakura Shinbei Kiln), 2025

Seiji Tea Bowl (Takakura Kiln), 2025

Yūichi Inoue, *Ro (Old Age)*, 1960, ink, paper. This artwork is in NIGO's personal collection. Created by the renowned 20th-century calligrapher Yūichi Inoue, the depicted ink character translates to 'old age', signalling NIGO's transition into a new stage of life.

Biographies

Rosa Abbott is Assistant Curator at the Design Museum, London. Her contemporary art background is complemented by a longstanding fascination with twentieth-century pop culture and material history. She has written for *Paper Visual Art*, *Hyperallergic* and *Aesthetica*, and authored catalogue essays for Hugh Lane Gallery, Garage Rotterdam and Château La Coste. She holds an MA in Culture, Criticism and Curation from Central Saint Martins and a BA (Hons) in English Literature/History of Art and Architecture from Trinity College Dublin.

Johanna Agerman Ross is the Conran Foundation Chief Curator at the Design Museum, London, where she oversees the exhibition programme, the permanent collection and the museum archives. She was previously curator of twentieth-century and contemporary furniture and product design at the Victoria and Albert Museum, London. In 2011 she founded the award-winning international design journal *Disegno*, now renowned for its in-depth, independent reporting on design, architecture, fashion and urbanism.

Tiffany Godoy is an editor and cultural strategist working at the intersection of fashion, media and image culture. Born in Los Angeles and based between Tokyo and Paris, she has worked across Asia, Europe and the United States since the late 1990s. A former Head of Editorial Content at *Vogue Japan* (2022–25), she writes and consults internationally on fashion and culture, and is the author of several books on Japanese street style.

Rachel Hajek is a curator, writer and researcher based in London. She is currently Curator at the Design Museum, London, having previously held positions at Tate Modern. She has contributed to numerous exhibitions and displays including, for the Design Museum: *Enzo Mari* curated by Hans Ulrich Obrist with Francesca Giacomelli, *Ai Weiwei: Making Sense*, and *Sneakers Unboxed: Studio to Street*.

Esme Hawes is a curator working across design in the twentieth and twenty-first centuries. She is currently Curator at the Design Museum, London, and has worked across projects such as *Charlotte Perriand: A Modern Life*, *WEIRD SENSATION FEELS GOOD: The World of ASMR* and the museum's *Platform* annual displays programme. She previously held positions at the Victoria and Albert Museum, London, working across a variety of international ventures and major exhibitions.

Tim Marlow is a writer, broadcaster and art historian. He is the Chief Executive and Director of the Design Museum in London.

W. David Marx is the Tokyo-based author of three books: *Ametora: How Japan Saved American Style* (Basic Books, 2015), *Status and Culture: How Our Desire for Social Rank Creates Taste, Identity, Art, Fashion, and Constant Change* (Viking Books, 2022), and *Blank Space: A Cultural History of the 21st Century* (Viking Books, 2025). His writing has also appeared in *The Atlantic*, *The New Republic* and *VOX*, as well as on NewYorker.com. He is now an outside director on the board of HUMAN MADE Inc.

Fiona McKay is a London-based curator. Following an MA in Fashion Curation, in 2013 she co-founded independent curatorial studio, White Line Projects, specialising in fashion-related exhibitions. In 2019 she joined the Centre for Sustainable Fashion. Fiona joined the Design Museum in 2022 as Assistant Curator, and has worked on exhibitions *REBEL: 30 Years of London Fashion*, *Splash: A Century of Swimming and Style* and *NIGO: From Japan with Love*.

Yuka Ryusenji has been a curator at the Sekisui Museum in Tsu, Mie Prefecture, Japan, since 1994. Contributing her expertise on Japanese art and ceramics, she oversaw the 2025–26 special exhibition *NIGO®* and *Handeishi*. The exhibition combined historical insight with thoughtful curation, connecting audiences with the rich heritage of Japanese craft.

Picture Credits

Every reasonable attempt has been made to identify owners of copyright. Any errors or omissions that are notified to the publisher will be corrected in subsequent editions.

Unless otherwise stated all images are credited as Photo Satoshi Nagare, courtesy of NIGO.

Credits listed here are by page number, with 'a' for above, 'b' for below, 'l' for left, and 'r' for right.

Cover: Photo Elliot James Kennedy © the Design Museum; pp. 2, 7, 16: Photo Elliot James Kennedy © the Design Museum; p. 18a: Courtesy NIGO; p. 18b: Dimitrios Kambouris/ Getty Images for Billionaire Boys Club; p. 19: Gregory Bojorquez/Getty Images; pp. 20–1: Photo Elliot James Kennedy © the Design Museum; pp. 24, 26: Courtesy NIGO; p. 27: Interior Design Wonderwall®. Photo Kozo Takayama; p. 98: Talaya Centeno/WWD/Penske Media via Getty Images; p. 101: Photo Toshio Ohno; p. 104: Courtesy NIGO; p. 106: Mo Wax Labels Ltd.; p. 107: Interview Magazine; p. 109: Courtesy NIGO; p. 158: Photo Thomas Thompson; p. 164: Photo Richie BWS; p. 165: Interior Design Wonderwall®. Photo Kozo Takayama; p. 166: Courtesy Louis Vuitton; p. 176: Francois Durand/ Getty Images; pp. 186, 187: Courtesy Louis Vuitton; p. 188l: Victor VIRGILE/ Gamma-Rapho via Getty Images; p. 188r: Peter White/Getty Images; p. 189: Victor VIRGILE/Gamma-Rapho via Getty Images; p. 190: Francois Durand/Getty Images; p. 191: dpa picture alliance/Alamy Stock Photo; p. 192: Photo Flo Kohl; p. 195: Photo Lukas Gansterer; pp. 199, 200, 201, 202: Photo Keiichi Sakakura.

Acknowledgements

Published to coincide with the first-ever retrospective of NIGO's work, held at the Design Museum, London, from 1 May to 4 October 2026, this book celebrates NIGO's vision and legacy.

Neither the book nor the exhibition would have been possible without the generosity of NIGO himself, who gave access to his extraordinary collection and archives, and participated in many curatorial and book-related conversations. We warmly thank him. We would also like to extend very grateful thanks to NIGO's team, for their much-appreciated support and for dealing patiently with many questions and deadlines.

This publication is the result of dedicated and focused collaboration between many individuals. We are extremely grateful to Pharrell Williams, TET Nishiyama and Fraser Cooke for sharing their thoughts in the Insight sections, and to W. David Marx, Tiffany Godoy and Yuka Ryusenji for their informative chapter texts. We are also grateful to Johanna Agerman Ross for her interview with NIGO, which was carefully transcribed by Margherita Dosi Delfini, and to Rosa Abbott and Fiona McKay for their invaluable text and caption work. Enriching the book with such engaging and inspiring texts, the combined insights and experiences of all the contributors have expertly set NIGO's career in context. We thank them all.

We thank Miranda Harrison for steering the book through the book's editiorial, design and production stages, and for editing the texts, and Rachel Prest for her eagle-eyed proofreading. Wayne Daly and Claire Lyon brought an accomplished design eye and skilful layout solutions to the book, and we are very grateful to them. We would also like to thank Anabel Navarro for her picture research and excellent negotiation skills.

The plate sections in each chapter feature specially commissioned photography of items in NIGO's collection. We are very grateful to NIGO for this unique set of photographs. We also thank F1 Colour and Gomer Press for their skilled colour work and print expertise, ensuring that every page and every object look their best.

The Design Museum is very grateful to the lenders of the exhibition, and to all of NIGO's collaborators over the years who have shared their time, expertise and stories with us for this project. We would like to thank the headline exhibition sponsor NOT A HOTEL for their generous support, and NIGO's chosen furniture partner, USM Modular Furniture.

We would like to conclude with a brief environmental note. The Design Museum is working hard to reduce its environmental impact across all its work. This publication was printed at Gomer Press, who use FSC-certified papers and low-energy XL106 presses. As a Carbon Balanced Printer, Gomer Press recycles aluminium plates and paper waste, and utilises solar energy installations.

Rachel Hajek and Esme Hawes

Design Museum Publishing
Design Museum Enterprises Ltd
224–228 Kensington High Street
London W8 6AG
United Kingdom

Designmuseum.org

First published in 2026

ISBN 978-1-872005-91-1

Front cover:
Portrait of NIGO at the Design Museum, London, 2026. Photo by Elliot James Kennedy. © the Design Museum

Back cover:
NOWHERE store signboard, 1993.
Photo Satoshi Nagare, courtesy of NIGO

Senior Publishing Manager:
Miranda Harrison

Publishing Manager:
Stefano Mancin

Curatorial Editors:
Rachel Hajek and Esme Hawes

Assistant Curatorial Editors:
Rosa Abbott and Fiona McKay

Copy-editing and proofreading:
Miranda Harrison and Rachel Prest

Designer:
Daly & Lyon

Picture Editor:
Anabel Navarro

Reprographics:
F1 Colour, London

Printer:
Gomer Press, Llandysul, Wales

Distribution:

Worldwide excluding USA and Canada
Thames & Hudson
181A High Holborn
London WC1V 7QX
United Kingdom
thamesandhudson.com

North America
ARTBOOK | D.A.P
75 Broad Street, Suite 630
New York, NY10004
United States of America
artbook.com